"Megan Smolenyak Smolenyak (besides having the coolest name I've ever heard) is the guru, the pope, the beginning, the middle and the end of genealogy. And like all good gurus, she inspires the rest of us to find our own roots, to keep digging until we know our own story. This book is an important book for anyone who has ever had a mother, a grandmother or a great-grandmother. Make it part of your library now."

Pam Grout
Author of *Art and Soul* and *Living Big*

"I won't try to tell you why your personal heritage is important. Read this book and you'll understand."

Beau Sharbrough
President, GENTECH

"In *Honoring Our Ancestors*, Megan Smolenyak Smolenyak beautifully captures the significance of remembering our roots. You'll want to get out your heirloom scrapbooks and artifacts to discover your legacy—or create a new tradition in your family. Connect with your history; give yourself the gift of your past with this book."

Cynthia Brian
Author of *Be the Star You Are!*
and co-author of *Chicken Soup
for the Gardener's Soul*

"One of the great shortcomings of America is that we idolize youth and minimize the value of the precious insight, intuition and wisdom our elders have to offer. The stories Megan shares in *Honoring Our Ancestors* give me hope that more of us are waking up to all we have to gain by paying attention and tribute to our forebears. By looking to the past, we can craft a better future."

Gerald Celente
Director of The Trends Research Institute
and author of *Trend Tracking, Trends 2000,*
and *What Zizi Gave Honeyboy*

D1016031

Honoring OUR Ancestors

Inspiring Stories of the Quest for Our Roots

Megan Smolenyak Smolenyak

Ancestry

Library of Congress Cataloging-in-Publication Data

Smolenyak, Megan.
  Honoring our ancestors : inspiring stories of the quest for our roots
/ Megan Smolenyak.
      p. cm.
  ISBN 1-931279-00-4 (pbk. : alk. paper)
  1. Genealogy--Anecdotes. I. Title.
  CS21 .S56 2002
  929'.1--dc21

                                          2002005752

Copyright © 2002
Megan Smolenyak Smolenyak

Published by Ancestry® Publishing, an
imprint of MyFamily.com, Inc.

P.O. Box 990
Orem, Utah 84059
www.ancestry.com

All Rights Reserved

All brand and product names are trademarks or
registered trademarks of their respective companies.

No part of this publication may be reproduced in any form
without written permission of the publisher, except by a reviewer,
who may quote brief passages for a review.

First Printing 2002
10 9 8 7 6 5 4 3 2 1

Printed in Canada

For Brian,
the gift I received for honoring my ancestors

Merry Christmas Mom!
I was really excited to find
this book for you, because
this is exactly what you do
more than anybody for our
family. Our Ancestors in
Spirit are always smiling
down on you for Honoring
them. Love, John xox

Contents

Acknowledgments

What a privilege it is to publish another book on a subject I love! And for this, I owe a debt of gratitude to two amazing women: my agent, Linda Konner, and Lou Szucs of Ancestry.com.

As with my last book, Juliana Smith, Julia Case, and Dick Eastman were kind enough to help me find incredible tales and Leland Meitzler generous enough to share some gems from Heritage Quest.

Stacy Neuberger once again provided invaluable help, making this a far better book than it would have otherwise been, and Seton Shields, Ray Freson, and Tom Neuberger endured rough drafts and furnished vital feedback and reality checks for which I am very grateful.

Jennifer Utley, Jennifer Browning, and Matt Wright patiently guided me through the editorial process, answering countless questions and accommodating a myriad of quirky situations. And Rob Davis did an amazing job on all the design aspects, creating a book I'm delighted to have my name on.

Janet Winter deftly handled all the attendant logistics so I could focus on writing and Anna Grace Harding was ever-present to remind me to occasionally do something other than write!

Many avid readers and fellow roots-seekers fed me a steady diet of stimulation and support as I lectured and book-stored my way across the country. Thanks for sharing your enthusiasm!

I am, of course, especially beholden to those whose inspiring stories appear in these pages. Thank you all for your willingness to share your tremendous ideas. Let's hope you have lots of imitators!

And finally, I would like to thank my still-new husband, Brian Smolenyak, who makes me wonder why I took so long to try this marriage thing! To explain all the support he gave me would require a book in itself, so suffice it to say, there's a little of him on every page. Thank you, Smokey.

Introduction

Would you believe me if I were to say that the ancient practice of ancestor worship is on the verge of becoming an integral part of your twenty-first century way of life? That this quiet phenomenon is already out there, assuming a thousand different forms? That it's just a matter of time until it's acknowledged, proliferates, and finds a way to tiptoe into your life?

When you actually ponder this premise, the evidence is everywhere you look. We probably just haven't noticed it because it doesn't exactly fit our Western paradigms and priorities. Our frantic, must-have-it-done-yesterday lives and obsessive focus on building better futures leave us little time for reflection on the past. *Ancestor worship? Isn't that something they do in China? We don't have time to build altars to folks who died generations ago. We're too busy living!*

But as more and more of us begin to question all this frenetic activity and the all-too-fleeting satisfaction it brings, we are searching for answers from other sources. And it just so happens that the past is a pretty good place to look when you're seeking guidance, inspiration, hope, and even role models.

The term "ancestor worship" may feel a little overstated to

many of us, so I've opted to refer to it as "honoring our ancestors" or occasionally as "ancestral tribute." But whatever you might choose to call it—ancestor worship, forebear fancy, roots-reverence, or some other phrase—the fact is that many of us have already fallen into some variation of this practice without even realizing it.

Take, for instance, the more than forty million Americans who identify themselves as genealogists. It's said that we stand on the shoulders of those who came before us, and roughly sixty percent of all Americans are interested in learning about the shoulders that gave them their boost. That's a third more than in 1995 and there are more roots-rookies every day.[1] Internet statistics tout genealogy as keeping company with sex and finance as the top online subjects, and at least two genealogical Web launches have crashed under the burden of traffic exceeding fifty million visits a day. [2,3]

Then there are the scrapbookers who are crafting heritage albums by the thousands. The size of this market grew six-fold during the last half of the 1990s and a new scrapbooking store opens every week in America.[4,5] Conferences have sprung up all across the country to accommodate demand and the Hobby Industry Association states that one in every five households now participates in scrapbooking.[6]

Want more evidence of our growing fascination with the past and those who lived it? How about the swelling popularity of antiquing and historical reenactments? And these are just the most obvious examples. As the stories in this book will reveal, countless other creative, ancestral tributes have been devised, sometimes in conjunction with one of these other pastimes and sometimes entirely solo.

The Quest for Roots

Once you delve into this world, you quickly discover that there are many different ways to honor our ancestors, and no matter how you might choose to do it, there is something inherently spiritual about it. Whether you do it for a sense of connection, to gain greater insight into who you are and why you're here, or for the sheer pleasure, the process itself is both invigorating and soul-soothing.

Many roots-seekers are looking for ways to simultaneously demonstrate respect and gratitude for their ancestors and to draw inspiration and direction from them. And encouragement to do so is even starting to creep into spiritual literature. Julia Cameron's book, *God Is No Laughing Matter*, touches on the subject when she declares, "Honoring our lineage honors ourselves. It deepens and strengthens our intuition ... A practice of quietly sitting and directly asking guidance from our elders often produces surprisingly specific and creative new directions."[7]

She then goes on to suggest that the reader construct an ancestors altar: "The creation of an ancestors altar is an Oriental tradition that would serve all of us very well ... Maintaining your ancestors altar ... will routinely put you in touch with your personal family energies. You will find yourself cherishing and respecting the unique creative coloration given to you by your ancestral roots."[8]

Although such shrines are among the better-known forms of ancestral tribute, the stories in this book will supply scores of alternatives, all of which can provide the grounding and direction that so many of us are either deliberately or unconsciously trying to find.

The Search for Identity

Just like spiritual seekers, those individuals on a genealogical quest are frequently motivated by a search for identity or self. Many feel that by turning to their ancestors, they can learn more about themselves. In fact, in a study of 1,348 genealogists conducted by a Canadian professor of Sociology, "to learn about my roots, about who I am" was the top reason given for conducting family history research. Fully eighty percent of those participating in the survey cited this incentive for their hunt.[9] Given the chance to elaborate, respondents made comments such as:

- [Genealogy] gives me an anchor in an otherwise very fluid world which is becoming more cold and impersonal all the time, and it gives me a solid foundation, a rock if you will, upon which to build and establish my identity as a person.

- I want to leave records for my children and grandchildren about the lives of those from whom they are descended. What quirks did they inherit from their ancestors: their dependence on liquor? their love of knowledge? their ability to work with their hands? their temper? their beauty? their shyness?

- Genealogy gives me a sense of continuity and . . . seems to answer the question of why I'm here.[10]

In such a transient world, many of us are looking to the past not only for a sense of identity, but also as a means to connect with others.

The Urge to Connect

Query a family historian about his or her motives, and contrary to old stereotypes, you will not find a person in search of illustrious roots or bragging rights. Instead, you will find someone hoping to connect with others, as evidenced by this typical response from the study mentioned earlier: "Genealogical research is a great 'leveler,' bringing people of all backgrounds together. And finding family relationships with them, unexpectedly, emphasizes what a small world we live in. Ultimately, we are all related if we could go back far enough."[11]

As one of the few forces in this world bringing people together, genealogy satisfies our hunger for connection and even expands our definition of "family." With the help of technology, the search for roots is triggering a worldwide, reverse diaspora, slowly undoing what centuries of migration has done.

Millions of roots-seekers are finding and reaching out to their third, fourth, and fifth cousins in what is rapidly amounting to a global game of tag. I find a distant cousin on the Internet and we feel an instant connection because we are kin. The blood, genes, quirks, personality traits, and predispositions of our common ancestors surface in some way in both of us, so the bond between us is effortless and almost instantaneous. This experience sparks my newfound cousin's interest in heritage-hunting, and before you know it, she's out there recruiting other distant cousins back into the clan. Our family may have been separated by oceans and centuries, but our tribal instinct is still intact.

Honoring Our Ancestors

The powerful combination of grounding, inspiration, identity, and connection that looking to the past can provide is at first an accidental bonus, but over time becomes, for many, as important as the pursuit itself. Even for those of us whose religious traditions incorporate and, to a certain extent, mandate some form of ancestral tribute, these spiritual benefits can come as a surprise.

With this dawning awareness and the intensifying cultivation of our forebears, is it any surprise that the last few years have seen an emergence of "ancestor tributes" in the West, that so many of us are emulating the centuries-old Asian tradition of honoring one's ancestors?

Writing on the exploding popularity of her area of expertise, feng shui authority Susan Chow points out that, "Acupuncture, tai chi, ch'i kung, and Chinese Traditional Herbal Medicine are a few of the Eastern practices that have now been embraced by the Western world. Just over a decade ago, most people would have chortled—or more probably just given the speaker a blank stare—at the mention of any of these practices. Today, however, the world has discovered that many of these ancient practices have considerable merits."[12]

Somehow it seems rather fitting that ancestor tribute should follow on the heels of feng shui since this ancient placement art was originally used for charting the most auspicious location to bury the dead. As Susan Chow explains, "It was believed that the location of the burial site of one's ancestors would have a direct influence on their descendant's Earth luck. As time passed, this practice was also applied to 'the houses of the living.'"[13]

And with our stubborn, not-invented-here mentality, isn't it equally as predictable that we would do with ancestor tribute exactly what we have done with feng shui; that is, put our finger prints all over it to make it "ours"? Feng shui specialist Helen Oon has noted, "The Western world has consumed this ancient wisdom with gusto and adapted it to the Western lifestyle." [14]

It is this beneath-the-radar phenomenon—the Western adaptation of this latest import, ancestral tribute—that the stories in this book will reveal. The tales that follow will show how we have already taken this ancient practice and made it indelibly and indisputably our own.

They will make it clear that ancestral tribute knows no age boundaries as the storytellers range from teenagers to a youthful gentleman of "eighty-seven-and-a-half." They demonstrate no gender divide as more than forty percent of the stories are told by men. They display no geographic predilection as the accounts come from people living from California to Iceland, and reflect experiences that occurred everywhere from Alaska to Ghana. They disclose no occupational tendencies as teachers, retirees, best-selling authors, students, realtors, filmmakers, accountants, and inmates number among the narrators. They divulge no ethnic proclivity as pockets of our Puerto Rican, Swedish, Native American, Jewish, Slovak, Africa-American, Scottish, Chinese, and Quaker heritage—just to name a few—are all represented. They don't even reveal a consensus on the definition of "ancestor," as some have somewhat unexpectedly chosen to pay tribute to near-contemporaries or people to whom they have no blood connection whatsoever.

If there is one common thread to all the stories, it is our endless well of creativity. These tales underscore that there is no "right" way to honor our ancestors, but rather, as many approaches as there are people with an inclination to do so.

It is my hope that you will use this book for an armchair shopping expedition and browse for ideas that inspire you. At the risk of abetting a crime, I encourage you to do your browsing with the intent of petty theft! Look for approaches you might want to steal and make your own. And should the fifty stories that follow leave you thirsting for more, be sure to turn to the epilogue for a menu of further inspiration!

Notes

1. Cuen, Lucrezia. "Roots Online: Americans Searching Web, Old Records, for Family Trees." ABCNEWS.com, 4 May 2000: "... one of an estimated 40 million Americans on the heritage hunt. A recent poll conducted by Maritz Research ... found interest in genealogy has climbed from 45 to 60 percent of all Americans over the past five years. One-third of those are actively searching out their roots ..."

2. Price, Christopher. "Hunt for family tree felled by log-on overload: Mormon church's genealogical website gets 50m hits an hour." *Financial Times*, 28 May 1999, p. 1: "The world's biggest genealogical website ... ground to a halt after hundreds of millions of users tried to log on. ... IBM said it was receiving up to 50m hits an hour...."

3. Koller, Mike. "Ellis Island Site Tops 1.5 Billion Hits." *Internet Week TechWeb*, 15 November 2001: "In the first six hours of its operation, the site let in only 8 million of about 50 million visitors before a crash program to install new alpha servers from Compaq and other technology rose to meet demand."

4. Ettenborough, Kelly. "Pretty Pages: Hobbyists Are Discovering the Joys of Keeping a Scrapbook." *The Arizona Republic*, 8 September 1998, p. D1: "According to the Hobby Industry Association, scrapbookers spent $50 million in 1995... At least one scrapbooking store opens each week in the United States, according to Creating Keepsakes."

5. Kruger, Jennifer Barr. "Scrapbooking—not just a passing trend." *Photo Marketing*, September 2000, Vol. 75, Issue 9, 23 pp: "By 1999, scrapbooking had grown to a $300 million industry, with no signs of slowing."

6. "Primedia Acquires Creating Keepsakes." *The Write News*, 7 March 2001: "According to the Hobby Industry Association (HIA), one in every five households participates in scrapbooking."

7. Cameron, Julia. *God Is No Laughing Matter: Observations and Objections on the Spiritual Path*. New York: Jeremy P. Tarcher/Putnam, 2000, p. 81.

8. Ibid., p. 82.

9. Lambert, Ronald D. "A Study of Genealogists & Family Historians – Part II." *The Global Gazette*, 1 January 1999, Vol. III, No. 1: "The most common reason for doing genealogy was to discover respondents' roots and identities. Fully 80 percent of the sample rated this an 'important' reason."

10. Ibid. All quotes excerpted from this article.

11. Ibid.

12. Chow, Susan. "The Real Stuff." *Feng Shui for Modern Living*, November/December 2001, p. 26.

13. Ibid.

14. Oon, Helen. "Stop! In the Name of Feng Shui." *Feng Shui for Modern Living*, November/December 2001, p. 11.

Photo courtesy of the Viking Trail Tourism Association (www.vikingtrail.org). Used with permission.

Sailing in His Trail

It's true that not everyone would think to build a Viking ship and sail it across the North Atlantic, but for me, it seemed a natural thing to do. I had always disliked the fact that there were no Viking ships in Iceland, because if it were not for them, we would not live on this island. After all, Iceland was settled by Vikings from present-day Norway around the ninth century. Since I had the know-how to build and sail such a ship, I decided to grab the opportunity.

I was born into a seafaring family, so the sea has always been my second home. At fourteen, I began working on fishing boats, and by twenty-five, I had been fully trained in the art and science of shipbuilding by my father and grandfather.

In 1994, I got the notion to build a Viking ship by myself and decided to use the ninth-century *Gaukstad* ship that had been excavated in Norway more than a century earlier as my model.

It took about eighteen months, but with the help of a ship-building friend, Thordur Haraldsson, the *Islendingur* (*Icelander*) was completed in May 1996. The resulting ship, constructed from oak and pine, was seventy-three feet long and weighed eighty tons.

Over and over during the construction process, I was stunned by the realization of how tremendously skilled the shipbuilders of the past were. Their craftsmanship and the development of the ships were nothing short of amazing. I would not have believed it if I had not experienced it for myself.

As the ship neared completion, I developed the idea of commemorating Leif Eiriksson's voyage to North America in the year 1000. As both an Icelander and a direct descendant of his, I had grown up listening to the Saga of Eirik the Red and the Saga of Greenlanders, medieval tales of the journeys of my ancestors.

The tales told how Eirik the Red was exiled from Norway for murder and settled into a farming life in the western part of Iceland. There, sometime around 975, his son Leif Eiriksson, known as Eirik the Lucky, was born. But history quickly repeated itself, and after another murder stemming from a feud with one of his neighbors, the Senior Eirik found himself expelled from Iceland for a period of several years. He used this time to pioneer settlement in Greenland and explore still further to the West.

Eirik the Red's tales of adventure apparently inspired his son, Eirik the Lucky, who then set out to explore on his own. Around the year 1000, he became the first European to ever reach the New World when he arrived in L'Anse aux Meadows, now a small fishing village in Newfoundland. These sagas were substantiated by scientific evidence when Norwegian archeologists uncovered remains of a Viking settlement at L'Anse aux Meadows in the 1960s. Historians now believe about ninety Norse men and women lived there for roughly ten years before returning home. Five hundred years later, Christopher Columbus made his claim to the continent, which Leif Eiriksson had dubbed Vinland the Good.

The millennial year of 2000 was approaching, so what better way and what better time to commemorate his voyage but to sail in Eirik the Lucky's wake exactly 1,000 years later? By doing this we would be paying tribute to his achievement. And who more appropriate to do this than one of his descendants?

It required a couple of years of planning, but on 17 June 2000, I left the little Icelandic port of Budardalur with a hardy crew of eight on board the sturdy *Islendingur* with the intention of recreating the 2,600 mile journey of my bold forebear. Many people asked me if we were afraid to cross the ocean on a Viking ship, but I trusted the ship completely and knew that if we treated it right, we had nothing to worry about. On the 28th of July, my confidence was rewarded when we sailed into L'Anse aux Meadows where we were greeted by an enthusiastic crowd of well-wishers who had come from all over Vinland the Good.

For me, sailing across the Atlantic was the fulfillment of a life-long dream. Seeing the land rising on the horizon brought to mind the relief and anticipation the Vikings must have felt after their long journey 1,000 years ago. I feel privileged to have been able to sail in their trail.

—*Gunnar Marel Eggertsson, Iceland*

Posterity for Posteriors

Many families have traditions and heirlooms they pass down through the generations—tall tales, jewelry, reunions, Bibles, and the like. In the Freas family, we've created a tradition and heirloom of an unexpected sort: a diaper.

To date, four generations of Freas descendants have had their pictures taken at the age of six months wearing the same cloth diaper. No one in our family knows exactly how or why this tradition was started, but we intend to keep it going. It serves as a reminder of our heritage, helps us bond with our ancestors, and gives the now dispersed Freas descendants a reason to stay in touch with each other.

The originators of this tradition were both born in Pennsylvania. Frank Dudley Freas was born in 1868 in

Hazleton, the fourth child of Dr. Henry Leigh Freas and his wife Amelia Gearhart Messenger Freas. Accounts of the Freas family in the late 1800s indicate that the family had a flair for the dramatic. Frank's oldest brother, Mordecai, was a magician known as the "Great Voxie," and Frank himself studied for the stage in Philadelphia following his graduation from Berwick High School in 1885.

It was in Philadelphia that he met Mary Agnes Sheahan. The story, as related to me by my great-aunt Jane Freas, is that Frank came to the Sheahan home to pick up the oldest Sheahan daughter for a date, but was smitten instead with Mary. Two years younger than Frank, Mary had intended to enter a convent, but changed her mind after making his acquaintance. She eventually convinced her somewhat reluctant parents to allow her to marry him, and Frank wed his "Irish rose" in Camden, New Jersey, in May 1889.

In November of that same year, Frank and Mary experienced the sorrow of losing their firstborn, a premature infant who survived a mere ten weeks. Their second child, Agnes (my grandmother-to-be), followed in June 1891. Perhaps it was the joy of seeing Agnes thrive that caused her parents to celebrate the arrival of the six-month anniversary of her birth by having a photograph taken of her wearing only a diaper. Unbeknownst to them, the seed of a tradition had been planted.

Frank and Mary subsequently had similar pictures taken of each of their other four children—all in the same diaper and all at the age of six months. This collection of five photographs was later mounted together and shows the diapered derrières of Agnes Amelia Freas (born 22 June 1891), Lois Gearhart Freas (born 21 February 1896), Betty Viola Freas (born 9 July 1899), Henry Leigh

5

Freas (born 4 May 1901), and Jane Kitchen Freas (born 23 August 1904). Apparently by the birth of the second child, the diaper had already been retired from its customary purpose and retained just for the use of these half-year milestone photos.

You would think that the diaper would have been misplaced during the fifteen-year dormant phase following the births in this first generation, but not in the Freas family! In 1919 when the first grandchild of Frank and Mary was born to their daughter Agnes and her husband, Thomas Hale Keiser, the peculiar family habit was resurrected. They also mounted their Freas diaper shots together, but with a two-generation twist: the frame contains photos of the Agnes Amelia Freas—the baby first photographed in 1891— and both of her children, Thomas Hale Keiser, Jr. and Mary Lois Keiser.

Still more Freas babies had their charms captured for posterity. Betty Jane Stahl, the only child of Leo Stahl and Lois Gearhart Freas Stahl, and Nancy Jane Waters, the only child of Frank Waters and Betty Viola Freas Waters, were next in line.

My generation made its contribution when my parents, Walter Maurice Culbert and Mary Lois Keiser Culbert, used the sexagenarian diaper to photograph their 1950s crop of Freas children: James Hale Culbert, Elizabeth Leigh Culbert, and Daniel Freas Culbert.

More recently, my wife, Kathleen Marie Mahoney Culbert, and I have kept the tradition alive with our own late-1980s trio of daughters and, of course, the durable Freas diaper. Clarissa Janes Culbert and twins Loralee Cummins Culbert and Annalisa Mahoney Culbert were the fourth generation photographed in the nearly century-old diaper.

Incidentally, while I have detailed the diaper's journey down my own direct line, I should point out that it is well-traveled, having crossed various state lines to grace the assets of various other sibling and collateral lines of Freas descendants.

The original framed photos of the children of Frank and Mary Freas were passed down to their youngest child, Jane. When Jane died, I was fortunate enough to receive them. I assembled them with the three more recent generations, and the four frames now hang together at my house as a constant reminder of the strength of family tradition, even if it is in the unconventional form of "diaper duty!"

—*James H. Culbert, Virginia*

7

Second Chances

Before prison, whenever I heard a set of keys rattling, I would think of a small child in church whose mother was trying to keep him or her quiet. Now that I'm in prison, there's a whole new meaning to that sound. To an inmate, that jangling means confinement, handcuffs, or an officer coming. Best to stop whatever you're doing and act like you're asleep.

After eleven years working on the Freedman's Bank Project, I often find myself wondering what the sound of keys meant to slaves. Do you think they too knew that the rattling of keys meant shackles and handcuffs?

One of the worst fears in the life of an inmate is being told, "Roll up, you're moving." Moving to a new housing unit is very uncomfortable because it means leaving old friends behind and not knowing what awaits you. I bet slaves felt the same anxiety when a new wagon or a stranger pulled up on a plantation. I believe they felt it even more so, because to them, it meant being sold or the loss of one of their loved ones. Inmates know what it's like being away from family, but our situation is usually temporary. For slaves, the separation was forever.

So what is this Freedman's Bank Project that has me trying to put myself in the shoes of slaves? Back in 1865, the Freedman's Bank Savings and Trust Company was established to help recently freed slaves with their financial dealings. It was supposed to be a safe place for them to deposit their money and protect it from swindlers, but due to bad management and just plain old fraud, the bank collapsed in 1874. More than $57 million in deposits was lost, dashing the hopes and dreams of the thousands who had trusted the bank.

The only good to come out of this was the records of the depositors. In order to open an account, a person had to give a lot of information, such as names of family members, places they had lived, and even details about relatives sold to other locations. Some 8 to 10 million African Americans have ancestors listed in these records, making them very valuable for those interested in tracing their roots, especially since there are so few records pertaining to slaves. The problem was that these records were never indexed in any way. With hundreds of thousands of files, it was unrealistic to even try to search for your family in them.

That's where we inmates come in. Back about a decade ago, I was one of four to enroll in the first genealogy class taught in the Utah State Prison system. One thing led to another and the South Point Family History Center was established in the prison. Although it was created with the assistance of The Church of Jesus Christ of the Latter-day Saints, the program is voluntary and open to people of all faiths. All inmates are eligible to participate as long as they honor center policies, such as not using bad language.

I was a diesel mechanic when I came to prison and hardly knew what a computer was, but I soon found myself serving as a project coordinator and becoming very skilled with computers. Word about the center spread and enthusiasm ran so high that it became difficult for me to schedule film reader time. Some inmates, while waiting for their allotted hour on the machine, were even seen holding up their microfilms to the light in an attempt to read them.

Shortly after the center opened, we were asked whether we might be able to help with some extraction projects, the idea being to transcribe and index information from microfilms so it would become more accessible to researchers. We immediately agreed.

During the 1990s we worked on a number of projects, but it was the Freedman's Bank Project that meant the most to us. And it was no small task. Eleven years, six hundred inmates, and over 700,000 volunteer hours later, some 480,000 Freedman's Bank records had been extracted and indexed. Now it's available for anyone who wants it on CD. What's in these records? Here's one example:

Record for:	Perry Jefry
Record Number:	3790
Date:	July 31, 1875
Where Born:	Warren County, Georgia
Residence:	Campbell Street on Savannah Road
Age:	24
Occupation:	Mattress making and cooking
Father:	Perry, killed by Ku Klux Klan
Mother:	Elizabeth
Brothers and Sisters:	Henry, William, Thoyda, and Austin. All four were killed by the Ku Klux in October nearly five years ago at

10

	Darcen near Thomson, Columbia County, Georgia
Notes:	I cannot write

Before we started, I had no idea the impact this work would have on me and the other inmates, but how can you work with records like this and not feel compassion? Time and time again, we found comments like:

"My father was sold."
"Brother killed, shot to death."
"Had a sister, she was burned to death."
"Father killed when I be little, crushed by wagon."

One record that will stay for me the rest of my life said, "I do not know what my daughter's name is. She was taken from me at birth and traded for some field tools." For me, one of the most important days of my life was when I held my first new-born daughter in my arms. I was so happy. I could not even begin to imagine what it would be like watching her traded for a handful of garden tools.

These records were teaching me compassion, empathy, sorrow, and concern for others. After each session I would go back to my cell and wait until the lights were off and I was alone. Then I would cry because there was a time when I, too, had mistreated people.

And I wasn't the only one affected. Even the toughest of us shed some tears when we saw how these people had been treated and what events took place in their lives. One Sunday when we were working on the records, I saw that the inmate sitting

11

next to me was crying. When I asked him if he was all right, he sniffled that he just couldn't believe how these people were treated. I reached out to comfort him and as I touched his shoulder, I noticed a tattoo on his neck that read KKK.

I really believe that God waited until now to have this work rediscovered because he knew what a great effect it would have on all those who worked on it. And while we can't compare our circumstances to theirs, I think that being in prison helped us relate to the slaves better than if we had done this work on the outside. In some small way, I feel as if we have given these silent voices a second chance to be heard, and we in return have been given our own second chance.

—*Blaine Nelson, Utah*

Photo courtesy of Kelden Peterson. Used with permission.

Tales from the Cemetery

Thirteen-year-old Kari Bowman shares her experience participating in a project arranged by Lucy Peterson who enjoys organizing a variety of church, 4-H, school and scouting events to help young people learn about their ancestors.

At first, I thought it was sort of strange when I heard that Mrs. Peterson was taking us to the cemetery for our activity—especially since there was still snow on the ground. But it made me curious when she gave us a list of questions to answer about the people buried there.

When we got there, we all got into groups and went around looking at the graves, answering the questions as best we could. It was fun to see whose birthday was close to ours and

13

who lived a long time and who didn't live long at all. We also looked for someone who was born and died around the same time of the year (like, born in late January and died in early February, even though there were a lot of years in between). We tried to find someone who lived without a spouse for a long time and someone who had the same initials or even the same name as we did.

Then some people dressed up and we went around to them as they stood by the graves. Some of them told stories as if they were the person in the grave and others told them as if they were the mother or a friend.

It helped me realize how people lived their lives back then. There were sad stories of people becoming sick and passing away and such. You could really tell how some of the people felt about those who died, such as the pain and sorrow the mother felt whose little two-year-old daughter had died. But you could also tell that she was happy that her baby was in a better place.

One story was about a girl who came West and then sent money to Ireland so her mother and sister could come, too. Her stepfather kept the letters and the money and she never heard from her mother. She had a really hard time here and was on her own and alone. Eventually her mother was able to come over to this area, but neither knew anything about where the other one was. Finally, someone figured it out and wrote to her to come see her mother before she died. She set out immediately, but only arrived as her mother was being buried. Then she stayed and raised a family here. She is the ancestor of some of my friends. It was very selfish of the guy who took the money, and good of the lady who figured out that they were both in America and took time to write the letter. It gave me a better appreciation for them and all the hard work and suffering they went through for us to be here.

I liked how we went around and heard the stories. I had heard of a few of the people in the cemetery because some of my friends whose families are from around here had a brother or sister buried there. I saw a lot of the names and realized that many of the people are related to my friends. It gave me a better background of our town.

It made me feel selfish in a way because I don't do as much for other people as they did for us. If it weren't for the people buried in this cemetery, their descendants wouldn't be here. It gave me a bigger appreciation for my own ancestors because I realized that if it weren't for them, I wouldn't be here either.

People who weren't with us might think it sounds a little strange, but I think it would be fun to visit the cemetery again and learn about different people than we did the last time.

—*Kari Bowman, age 13, Utah*

Tanks for the Memories

My family tree includes Tories from the Revolutionary War and Confederate regimental commanders from the Civil War. My grandfather was a submariner in World War I, and my father was an infantry officer in World War II. With such deep military roots, I suppose it's not surprising that I collect military memorabilia even though I never served. But most collectors don't need a 150,000 square foot warehouse to store their prized possessions.

It started, as these things often do, when I was a kid. I would go to shows with my dad and buy the odd canteen or medal. This led to participation in reenactments of Civil War, World War I, and World War II battles. It wasn't until the mid-1990s that I took the step that marked the point of no return: the purchase of a beat up M-3A1 half-track I found in someone's backyard. After that, it was a slippery slope to the acquisition and restoration of assorted tanks, armored cars, self-propelled guns, artillery, and more half-tracks. I began traveling the world, scouring scrap yards in cities with unpronounceable names, looking for that next addition to my motor pool.

Before long, it became clear that this was more than a hobby, so I invested in the necessary equipment and facilities to establish "Combat Vehicles" in nearby Easton, Pennsylvania. Now we provide authentic military vehicles and do consulting work for films, documentaries, reenactments, and commercials. From the annual recreation of the Battle of the Bulge, the largest land battle ever fought by the U.S. Army, in Fort Indiantown Gap, Pennsylvania, to the premiere of the movie *Godzilla* in New York, our vehicles are there.

Why do I do it? For the memories. Every military vehicle has a history—what it did in combat, what it witnessed and survived, and the stories of its operators. I deliberately seek out veterans, the former partners of these vehicles, and sometimes they find me. I love listening to these men, (now in their seventies and eighties) talk about what happened to them sixty years ago.

I get to hear history firsthand—all the horrors of war, but also the funny stories. One veteran who had served with General McAuliffe at Bastogne where they were surrounded by Germans confirmed that McAuliffe, apparently a very devout and disciplined man, really did reply, "Nuts!" when presented with a demand for the Americans' surrender. He added the detail that the general had turned bright red and walked away, as he always did when angered, but insisted that no stronger language ever

Above: photo copyright Jim Jamman Below: photo copyright Jim Gilmore. Used with permission.

In 1945, George Kassel and Jim Jamman posed on a recently captured German tank. Fifty-seven years later, Jim revisited his past by striking the same pose on a recently restored Jagd Panzer Hetzer 38T from Michael Moss's collection.

escaped his lips. What an experience to speak with an eyewitness to this colorful and important moment of our history!

On another occasion, I was part of a group participating in the Battle of the Bulge reenactment. Our American-made tank had broken down and we were all cold, angry, and griping. A jeep pulled up with an imposing, seventy-ish gentleman at the helm. He loudly berated us, bellowing, "I never saw a German tank that worked. They were always broken down and shot up. Who are you to be bellyaching when you're in an American one?" We were all a little more willing to accept the uninvited comments when we learned they were coming from Col. David E. Pergrin, Commanding Officer of the 291st Combat Engineers, whose tenacious unit had been so key in the original battle.

The most rewarding aspect of my hobby-business, though, is seeing the reactions of the average soldiers who served in relative anonymity. Most of these fellows think no one remembers what they did, and they say their kids could care less. They love what we're doing here and usually have to choke back a few tears. Time changes their perception. They always think the vehicle is so much larger or smaller than it seemed way back then, but the attachment never wavers. It recently took me twenty minutes to get an eighty-eight-year-old vet into the tank in which he had served, but it was worth it to see the broad smile that spread across his face.

Even more unforgettable was the time a group of veterans came for what was to be a half-hour visit and stayed five hours reminiscing about this crucial chapter of their lives. That evening, one of them had a stroke and passed away. I only learned when his family called to express their gratitude that he was able to spend his last hours reliving the most memorable part of his life. It's experiences like this that continue to fuel my dedication to collecting oversized artifacts of military history and the stories of the men who served in them.

—*Michael D. Moss, Pennsylvania*

Ancestors in Training

Don't you wish your ancestors had left more of a trace, more clues about the times in which they lived, more hints about what they were like as people? We do. So when we decided a few years ago that it was time to "put our affairs in order," we were curious to learn about the cyber cemetery option.

It's human nature to have an aversion to accepting the fact that you're going to die someday, but we crossed that bridge a long time ago when our parents passed away. Having gone through this experience, we wanted to look a little forward so our kids wouldn't have to worry. It's not as if we sit around thinking about dying; we're not morbid about it. We just thought it would be a good idea to tend to this while we could still make our own decisions.

But we soon found ourselves faced with a bit of a dilemma. Although we had determined some time ago that we wanted to be cremated (because we don't want to take space that's needed), we still wanted some way to be remembered even if it would be without the traditional burial plot.

When we called nearby Bellerive Cemetery, they told us about an area with a chapel, pond, and garden that was set aside for people who were cremated, but wanted to leave a remembrance. It sounded like a good fit, but we became even more convinced when they told us about the Forever Enterprises services.

This company creates videos—memorial biographies—of people's lives that can be viewed either at special kiosks at the cemetery or on the Internet. Apparently, it was started by the Cassity brothers whose family has long been in the funeral business. When they discovered an old audio cassette of their grandmother, they realized how much they had already forgotten about her—her laugh and the inflection of her voice. So they developed this idea to try to capture the essence of people's personalities, rather than just the usual name and birth and death dates found on tombstones.

Sometimes these digital biographies are commissioned after the fact by grieving family members who want a fitting memorial for a deceased loved one, but we preferred to make our own biography ahead of time so we could be remembered the way we wanted to be. We reasoned that when parents die, it's naturally a distressing time. In many instances, they've been ill for some time and are not the vigorous person of one's memories. We didn't want that to be the last impression we left. Instead, we wanted to leave a lively picture of our-

21

selves, our voices, and maybe even a small piece of our personalities.

So we gathered up some of our favorite photos—the two of us at various ages, our parents, our kids, and so forth—and taped a narrative describing each of them. In addition to these pictures and commentary, we chose to have a video produced. Our interviewer for this mini-documentary guided us through a series of questions that made us realize how much history we had seen and taken for granted. We remember outside toilets and streetcars, for instance, but we hadn't registered that this would be news to our children and grandchildren.

All of this was edited into an eleven-minute video—we were very impressed with what you can do by simply combining some audio and visuals. With Nat King Cole's "Unforgettable" playing softly in the background, the finished biography actually provoked a few tears, but the overall tone is very upbeat. When you view it, you can see that we're enjoying ourselves. You certainly don't get a visual image of folks with one foot in the grave!

Still, we were reluctant to tell our friends because it's a little like getting a new car. You don't want to go to your neighbor and say, "Hey, look at my new car!" It's just too egotistical, but if people ask, we're happy to elaborate and show them our video. All of our friends who have seen it think it's cool, but none of them have done it themselves yet. Perhaps they're not ready to confront their own mortality or are a little squirmy about this notion of speaking from beyond the grave.

That's fine with us. We realize we're on the ground floor with this, that we're pioneers of a sort, and we're interested to see how it goes. For now, we're content that our children, grandchildren, and even unborn Kuny descendants will be able to see us as we truly are, and not simply as frozen images in some old photos. And we like to think that our progeny will appreciate our efforts to be good ancestors by thinking ahead to the days they might want to learn more about us. We only wish that our ancestors had been able to do this for us!

—*Pat and Ken Kuny, Missouri*

Photo courtesy of Lisa See. Used with permission.

On Gold Mountain

I grew up hearing wonderful, though often strange, stories about my family. Fong See, my great-grandfather, came to the United States from China in 1871. Only fourteen upon arrival, he quickly adjusted to his new surroundings in Sacramento, California, and started a business specializing in "fancy underwear for fancy ladies." In a move that was not only unusual but also illegal at the time, he married a white woman, Ticie Pruett. Since marriages between "Mongolians" and whites were against the law, my great-grandparents had a contract drawn up to seal their union. Together, the enterprising couple shifted the focus of the business to Chinese curios and antiques and built a small dynasty after resettling in Los Angeles. Due to his success and longevity, living as he did to 1957 and the age of one hundred, Fong See was viewed as a patriarch not only of his own family but of Los Angeles Chinatown.

24

This much I knew since I spent much of my childhood at our family store in Chinatown listening to my grandmother and great-aunt Sissee tell stories about Fong See. Others knew, too, and would occasionally approach our family about interviews for articles, screenplays, or documentaries. But always the family said no. I think this was because they were arrogant on the one hand (why should we participate in someone else's project?) and embarrassed on the other (since so much of what had happened was against the law).

This is how things stood until 1989 when one of my cousins, Auntie Sissee's daughter, approached me and said, "Mom has some stories she wants to tell you." Perhaps it was her recent eightieth birthday that prompted Auntie Sissee to open up, but whatever the reason, I learned details I had never known.

Fong See had had four wives, not two. He also wasn't the first in our family to come to the "Gold Mountain," as America was referred to by Chinese immigrants, who spoke of streets lined with gold. In fact, he had come in search of his father, Fong Dun Shung, who had emigrated a decade earlier to work on the building of the transcontinental railroad and then vanished. This left the family so destitute that my great-great-grandmother back in China was forced to carry people on her back between villages to make a living. Finally, Auntie Sissee mentioned a subject so forbidden that I'd never heard a word about it before: the kidnapping of several of Fong See's nephews. So my family history was even more entertaining—and secretive—than I had known! I envisioned an article or maybe a ten-page family history to include with that year's Christmas card.

Sadly, Aunt Sissee died just two months after deciding to share these long-held secrets, but by speaking to me, she had tacitly granted permission to the rest of the extended family not to be afraid of the truth of our family history. At Aunt Sissee's funeral banquet, an assortment of aunts, uncles, and cousins offered to share their pieces of the family puzzle with me. Accepting their invitations, I soon realized I was dealing with much more than a Christmas card insert.

After half a decade of research and writing, *On Gold Mountain*, an honest retelling of the one-hundred-year odyssey of my Chinese American family, was published to reactions I had never imagined. As I was writing, I often wondered whether there was really anyone out there who was going to care. Most of us are fascinated by our own family histories, but would total strangers care about mine? Today, the book is in its ninth American edition and has been translated into five other languages. Now, after all these years, I think I know why people connect to it.

On Gold Mountain works because we haven't really learned Chinese American history in this country. We go through school never seeing a mention of the Chinese Exclusion Act of 1882, which barred the immigration of Chinese to the United States. Readers are stunned to learn that Chinese were not permitted to become naturalized citizens, own property, or marry Caucasians. For many people, just to learn this history is a real shock.

But beyond that is the universality of my family's story. In almost all of our family trees, we have someone who was brave enough—sometimes crazy enough—to leave his or her home country to come to this land of dreams. For us to be here today, there had to be people before us who struggled, endured, failed, succeeded, triumphed.

Photo by Karen TenEyck courtesy of Lisa See. Used with permission.

It is these connections I hope to help others make, and it seems as if my family story is determined to assist me by finding fresh outlets and means to have itself told. I never expected to find myself in the role of curator or libretto-writer, but *On Gold Mountain* is now both a museum exhibit and an opera. "On Gold Mountain: A Chinese-American Experience," an exhibition organized by the Autry Museum of Western Heritage, recently traveled to the Smithsonian where more than 640,000 people explored the bits and pieces of my family's adventures in America. The history of Los Angeles Chinatown and the larger history of Chinese Americans in general are brought to life through the possessions of six generations of the See family. The feedback sparked by the exhibit—simple comments such as, "My family came from Italy, but used the same kind of clothes iron as yours"—confirm the power of family history as a means of helping people relate to our nation's history.

Through the medium of opera, I told a more emotional version of my family's story, focusing on the love between my great-grandparents, Fong See and Ticie, who eventually separated but never stopped loving each other. Each artistic form I have had the opportunity to explore has allowed me to see a different aspect of my family story and has encouraged others to consider their own family sagas. I was thrilled to learn that something about the opera—perhaps its core story of a fragmented family so familiar to many today—touches young people.

Recently, I learned that *On Gold Mountain* is being used as a means to get students in Los Angeles schools to talk about racism. I have even heard of college applicants citing the book, exhibit, or opera as their inspiration for selecting Asian-American studies as their major. I certainly never expected any of this to happen, but I take pride in all these ripple effects from Aunt Sissee's original request. My family left me a remarkable legacy, which I hope to pass on by helping others recognize and appreciate the hidden treasures in their own family histories.

—*Lisa See, California*

My Mother's Example

When I think about honoring one's ancestors and the many images that conjures up, foremost in my mind is my mother. When my brother, sisters, and I were younger, it was always a source of humor to tease our mother for turning to the obituary page first when she picked up the daily newspaper. Front-page news always came second to the back-page obituary section in my mother's morning routine.

"Oh my word," she'd sigh, "so-and-so's mother-in-law passed away."

"Who's that?" one of us would question, not bothering to look up from the comics section of the paper or the far more interesting facts from the box of cereal perched close to our face.

"You remember her, we met her at her grandson's wedding. She was such a nice lady. It's really such a shame. She was only seventy-two."

"Mom!" one of us would say. "You met that woman once, six years ago!" And the rest of us would start to laugh.

"Well, it may have been only once, but she was very nice anyway, and I'm sure her family will miss her," Mom would defend.

Mom is on a first name basis with most of the major funeral directors in our city since she attends every wake service or funeral of any acquaintance she can.

"Oh, I see Bill has Mrs. Smith," she'd say as she reads the obituary. "I'll have to remember to bring along some of those Italian knots I just made when I go to the funeral home tonight. His little boy just loves those cookies."

It doesn't matter to Mom if she doesn't personally know the person who died. If they were a relative of a friend, or even a friend of a friend, she won't hesitate to thumb through her ready supply of sympathy cards, pick out just the right verse, pen some appropriate sentiment at the bottom, and send it out in that day's mail.

When a neighbor or close friend passes away, it is our mother who shows up at their door with a tray full of much appreciated, homemade Italian cookies, followed by warm hugs and sincere condolences for their loss. Then, at just the right moment, my mom will share some story or anecdote about the recently deceased person, which never fails to bring a smile to their loved one's face as they fondly reminisce.

But perhaps what mom is most noted for is her Memorial Day Pilgrimage. Annually, over the Memorial Day weekend, she travels to half a dozen cemeteries to visit the gravesite of every one of our deceased family members. Like most people, Mom does the traditional planting of flowers, or hanging of a wreath, but as she carefully beautifies each plot, she casually begins to talk to each of our ancestors, bringing them up-to-date on the latest family happenings.

"Davey's starting college this fall, Mummy," she said last year at my grandmother's grave. "You'd be so proud of him. He's grown into such a fine young man."

Now, as a child of ten or eleven, nothing seemed more mundane than to accompany my mother all over the countryside and watch her talk to tombstones. I used to think she was positively obsessed with death. "How can you do this?" I'd ask her while I stood nearby with my arms clenched tightly around my chest. "Don't graveyards give you the creeps, Mom?"

"Don't be silly, Jodi," she'd reply. "These are my aunts and uncles and my grandparents—your great-grandparents. They're our family, and there isn't anything frightening about our family."

I didn't fully understand my mother's devotion until I grew up and found myself picking up some of her habits like baking cookies or sending off a sympathy card. Once I came to see the genuine appreciation of my simple gestures in the eyes of my recipients, I realized that my mother's real obsession was not with death, rather, it was her desire to lend comfort to the living by honoring their dead.

This realization was profoundly illustrated to me when I had to bury my infant daughter three weeks after her premature birth. Being so completely devastated at the time, I couldn't think straight, let alone make any arrangements. Thankfully, my mother was by my side. Without hesitation, she quietly handled every detail, right down to arranging for Hayley to be buried in a small portion of her own plot, overlooking the beautiful mountains of our small Pennsylvania town. I had no words to thank her at the time, but Mom wasn't seeking thanks or recognition. She just wanted to comfort me, her baby, as I grieved for the loss of my own. Her strength saw me through the most painful time in my life, and in her words, "that's what family is all about."

Several years later, when I moved to Wisconsin, it was very difficult for me to leave Hayley behind. It helped that I believe my daughter is an angel, who I carry with me always in my heart, and whose spirit guards over her twin sister and new baby brother. But what comforts me most is the knowledge that my mother is keeping watch over my baby, just as she does my grandparents, aunts, and uncles. With quiet gentleness, and perfect respect for our loved ones who have passed on, my mother sees to it that no one is forgotten, no one is neglected, and our family lives on.

I have learned through experience that there is no truer way to honor our ancestors than through the example of my mother, Beverly Ann (DeSantes) Iachini, who pays tribute to those who are no longer with us by loving and caring for the ones they've left behind.

—Jodi L. Severson, Wisconsin

Genetically Predisposed

I was the kid in school who had his genealogy chart already prepared when the teacher thought to assign a family history project. I can't remember when I became interested in genealogy, but "family" has always meant something special—perhaps because we didn't have much family in my hometown.

A couple of years ago, while browsing through an online database, I spied a name that was of interest to me. The potential treasure, the surname of one of my great-grandfathers, was on www.jewishgen.org's Family Finder. Like any self-respecting genealogist (thirty-nine years and counting), I wrote an introductory e-mail to start a dialogue and see what the Argentine who had posted the message might know.

This new contact prompted me to look for additional information about this particular ancestor, born in the 1850s on the Yalta peninsula in Ukraine, but translating exit passports and wedding documents didn't move the search forward as hoped. After several e-mail exchanges with members of two branches of the possible relatives in Argentina, failure to locate critical census information for the Eastern Crimea, and the inability to make any link to the information supplied from Argentina, I was very disappointed and frustrated.

I had been told that the records were either lost during World War II or were simply not to be found. Another dead end in my genealogy—and this time I suspected I was very close. The Argentine family had immigrated to Argentina in 1913, just four years after my great-grandfather moved to the U.S. Two of their children had names identical to those of my grandmother's siblings, and my grandmother and one of their great-aunts shared the same name. They even had a story about relatives coming to America. We had geography, naming conventions, and surnames in common, yet the paper trail was cold.

I believe that honoring one's ancestors means never giving up the search, so there was no question of simply quitting. I racked my brain for possibilities. A few years earlier, I had read several articles about a DNA project conducted at the University of Arizona that had reverse engineered the Cohanim gene. In that study, Arizona's Dr. Michael Hammer had tested a few hundred men who claimed to be Cohanim, whom Jewish tradition accepts as direct descendants of the biblical Aaron. The results of that study showed that a statistically significant percentage of people who believed they were Cohanim by oral tradition actually shared a genetic signature.

The power of that initial success story excited my genealogically tortured mind. The memory of that article and the thought of how I might be able to use DNA for my own family studies flashed like a sought after surname on a white piece of paper being projected by a bright light in a dark cubicle in Salt Lake City's Family History Library.

I dashed off an e-mail to Buenos Aires: "Can you please coerce some male Nitz to take a simple DNA test?" Answer: "I'm a Nitz woman. This is no problem."

Now I had to find an appropriate male from the United States. Since my connection to this great-grandfather was on the maternal side, I was not qualified to provide the American Nitz sample. In fact, there was only one cousin who would be a suitable candidate. Luck of the genes! I called my cousin—whom I had never met—and found he was not home. When I called back the next day, he was working on the car. During the third call, I explained to his wife what I was trying to prove. She said she doubted that he would want to take a DNA test, but she thought this was very exciting and was sure her powers of persuasion would prove successful. They were.

A quick search of the Internet produced listings for two men by the name of Michael Hammer in the geneticist's hometown. I dialed the second one for no apparent reason. He was on his way to the airport, but came to the phone. I had called to request Y chromosome DNA testing (passed from father to son down through the generations). Barring that, I intended to ask for the name of a lab that could perform this type of test between the only living male descendent of my maternal great-grandfather and a male descendent of the possible relatives in Argentina.

While the Dr.'s "no" was understandable given the nature of university research, I have been known to be a persistent fellow. During our conversation, I learned that no commercial facility in the world currently conducted the type of testing I needed. While quizzing him about my options, I heard an inspiring and heartening response from Dr. Hammer, "I get calls like this all the time. Someone should start a business."

Sensing his desire to help, but lacking the will to be side-tracked from his own research, I asked if the university could perform work on my behalf—potentially as a business on a for-profit basis. The words just came out of my mouth.

As a genealogist, I could see this as a potential door through the proverbial brick wall. I saw a paradigm shift caused by DNA testing in my family history world. I spent the weekend putting my thoughts on paper, and then sent them to the folks at Arizona. About a month later, I received positive news from the university.

During our proof of concept phase, we used fifteen different case studies, some with known answers and some based on solid, genealogical hunch. I am happy to report that the person in Argentina and my distant cousin in California matched perfectly on the DNA test that was to become the standard offering by the company I never planned to build—but build it every day we do!

In early 2001, I went to Argentina to spend a few days with my family. During the course of those days I met about twenty family members. The meetings were great, informal, and of course highly memorable. We still don't know if their great-great-grandfather and my great-great-grandfather were brothers or first cousins, but I know that I'm welcome at their dinner table and they're welcome at mine!

—*Bennett Greenspan, Texas*

To learn more about DNA testing for genealogical purposes, visit www.familytreedna.com.

More Than Child's Play

I began researching my roots in late 1994, shortly after retiring. I realized that I knew nothing about my heritage, and I decided to start querying assorted cousins. Regrettably, they weren't able to tell me much more than I already knew. My parents had divorced when I was only two years old and my mother never spoke about my father, whom I had only seen twice in my life. My mother and grandmother had died, so I was at a loss as to what to do next.

A friend stepped in and offered to do a surname search in an online phone database and printed out several pages of Semancik/Semanick/Semanik/Semanek/Semanchik names. I wrote letters to all of them—more than three hundred in total. The first breakthrough was a response from Mary Semanick, who turned out to be an unmarried cousin from Pennsylvania. Her father, along with six of his brothers and sisters, had immigrated from Olsov, located in eastern Slovakia. Their immigration began in 1886 and ended in 1930. With the help of this cousin, I was able to ascertain that my grandfather, Carl John Semancik, was the first of these siblings to immigrate. He was the oldest in the family and settled in the Hazleton area near Wilkes-Barre, Pennsylvania. All the other siblings who survived to adulthood followed.

My grandfather changed his name to Semanick, married, and started a family in the late 1800s. Like many others living in that time and place, he worked as a coal miner and participated in strikes. During a scuffle in one particular strike, he hit one of the security guards and knocked him down. Not knowing whether the man was dead or merely knocked out, union offi- cials secretly sent him out of state to Cascade County, Montana, where he again went to work in the mines. Effectively separat- ed from the rest of his clan, Carl, who began using his middle name of John, eventually lost touch with them.

With great persistence, I slowly managed to find cousins descending from all the brothers and sisters of my grandfather. From research in church records, I learned that there were at least fourteen children in the immigrant generation. Six died young and the others—Carl, Thomas, Agnes, Stephen, John, Dorothy and Baltasar—all ventured to America. Today, their descendants live in California, Idaho, Ohio, Pennsylvania, New Jersey, New Mexico, and Arizona.

But I had not yet discovered all this information in 1998 when I made plans to go to Slovakia to learn more about my family. I traveled to Levoča, about twenty miles from Olsov, and made contact with Vladimir Flak, a local genealogy guide.

Cyril Semancik, Baltasar and Anna's youngest son

Vlado took me to two archives where we were able to find information on the youngest brother, Baltasar, the last of the family to leave Slovakia in 1930.

The next natural step was to visit Olsov, population 480, and meet with the mayor, Albin Bucko. The mayor examined the documents I had brought, including a passport of Anna, the wife of the youngest immigrant, Baltasar. Scrutinizing the paper, he exclaimed, "Bucko, Bucko!" and pointed to himself. His name and Anna's maiden name were the same. After comparing notes, we determined that we were related through Anna. I was thrilled to discover that the first person I had met in the village—the mayor, no less—was my relative!

I was taken to visit several other relatives and then to meet one of the older men in the village. It was thought that this fellow might remember the family from the 1930s. I showed him five passport pictures of Baltasar, his wife Anna, and their three children. Gingerly handling one of them, the old man's face broke out in a big smile. "Cyril, Cyril," he said, pointing to a photo that was indeed of Cyril Semancik, Baltasar and Anna's youngest son. This elderly man and Cyril had been playmates and he sadly recalled the day the Semancik family left for America. He knew then that they would never see each other again.

I asked why the boys hadn't written to each other, but the mayor explained that those who immigrated never stayed in contact. I thought this was a shame and I wanted to try to make amends. Wandering around the village, it struck me that conditions weren't much cheerier today for the children of Olsov than they must have been for the separated playmates of

39

seventy years ago. Not one home had any toys or equipment in the yard for children. I noticed children sitting in front of several houses with nothing to do, and I was determined to find a way to let these children know that someone cared.

When I arrived back in the United States, I knew exactly what to do. I launched a campaign to raise funds for playground equipment for the children of Olsov by contacting descendants of all the Semancik siblings who had emigrated to America. Every branch pitched in and the money was soon collected. I carefully sketched out how each of the donors' roots extended back to the Semancik family in Olsov. Fortuitously, one of the newly found cousins was making a trip to Europe and agreed to take the money I had collected to the mayor. Ed and Bernice Kirby found themselves treated like royalty in Olsov and were shown the schoolyard where the equipment would be installed.

The mayor was elated at this powerful act of kindness from descendants of a family who had left the village seventy to a hundred years ago. He said he could never imagine something like this ever happening. In our honor, a plaque was recently erected at the playground acknowledging the contribution of the Semanick clan.

But I'm not done yet. My latest project? I arranged for a Peace Corps worker in Slovakia to go to Olsov and find out how many children between the ages of five and eight live in the village. Forty coloring books and crayon sets will soon be on their way to these children. These children may be grateful for their unexpected presents, but I am the one who has been blessed. Without question, finding my scattered family and returning to my family's homeland has been the highlight of my life. What a pleasure it is to be doing the most rewarding "work" of my life in my retirement!

—*Pete Semanick, New Mexico*

A Stitch in Time

Almost everyone in America is here because of the bravery and adventurous spirit of our predecessors. In my case, four people—two men and two women—decided to leave their Swedish homeland, families, friends, churches, and surroundings for a foreign land of unfamiliar people, language, and customs.

Anna Sofia Johansson, eighteen years old on 5 September 1889, and her fiancé, twenty-three-year-old Axel Albert Lindahl, traveled from their homes in Mjölby, Östergötland to Göteborg, Sweden. They boarded the S.S. *Romeo* the next day and started their voyage to North America. Several years later, Karl Nilsson, twenty-one, from Ör, Dalsland, having served his military obligation, embarked for "Nord Amerika" on 21 July 1892 from Göteborg on the S.S. *Ariosto*. In 1895, Anna Kajsa Eriksdotter, twenty-two, her younger brother and widowed mother left their home in Lerhol, Värmland for the journey to

Chicago, Illinois, to join three older brothers. Anna's party went to Oslo, Norway, boarded the S.S. *Angelo*, and sailed on September 6th.

All three ships sailed to Hull, England, the main gathering place for Scandinavians on their way to the United States. Once there, the emigrants rode the railroad to Liverpool and boarded transatlantic steam ships to the United States. Anna and Axel steamed to Boston, Massachusetts, on the S.S. *Catalonia* while Karl and Anna traveled to Ellis Island on the S.S. *Majestic* and S.S. *Campania* respectively.

After arriving in Boston, Anna and Axel moved to Brockton, Massachusetts, where they married and had the first of their seven children. They eventually settled in Chicago, Illinois, where the last four children were born. The youngest, my mother, Violet, was born in 1906.

Karl arrived at Ellis Island only eight months after it opened. Deciding against farming to become a carpenter, he went to Chicago. There he changed his name to Charles H. Nelson and got his first job working on the 1893 World's Exposition.

Anna and her party arrived in New York and boarded the train for Chicago where the older brothers had jobs and a home. Some years later, Anna met Karl at church. The immigrant couple married in 1903, and had a son, Ewald, in 1904. Ewald, my father, was followed by two sisters.

These amazing people, so young and full of adventure, led very active and fulfilling lives in their new homeland. So many of us take it as a simple fact that our forebears made the journey, but I often ponder whether I would have had the courage to do the same. What would it take to make you do something that extreme?

The quilt depicts the journey from Sweden to America

I love family history and have wanted to share the knowledge of my bold grandparents with my children. I also love designing and creating quilts, so I decided to combine my two pastimes and make a genealogy quilt—one that would commemorate the daring decision my grandparents made to leave their homes, venture to a new land, and launch a new way of life.

Out came the paper, pencil, crayons, and maps and into the stereo went Mozart and Rachmaninoff as I started designing the quilt top. Being intrigued by history, geography, biography, and archeology, I wanted to infuse the quilt picture with all of these disciplines.

Since the travelers came from Sweden, I needed to put that in the upper right or northeast corner. They went to the United States, so that needed to be toward the lower left or southwest corner. I wanted to show the difference in size between the two countries, so I reduced and enlarged various maps until I had both Sweden and the United States to the same scale, but then I realized I could only show the Boston-New York area of the United States because it's just too big! England and Ireland were only stopovers on the journey, so they're not to the same scale.

To depict the ocean, I wanted shades of blue with a wave pattern, and for the land, I wanted greens and browns that looked like hills, rocks, and trees. A challenge. I was off to the fabric

43

stores. For several months I kept looking, buying a remnant here and the odd swatch there until I had a large assortment.

I sewed nine different fabric pieces into each block to make up the ocean area, then cut the piece to form a "bending river" of ocean with very light blue areas on either side. In the pale blue areas, I hand-embroidered genealogical information about my parents, brothers, and me, and our children and grandchildren. In the Sweden area, I embroidered the towns and provinces of my grandparents as well as the ports of Göteborg and Oslo. In England and Ireland, the port names of Hull, Liverpool, and Queensland and the actual route of the railroad tracks were carefully stitched. And of course, the names of towns and states where the immigrants arrived in the United States are also embroidered on the quilt top.

In a border, a place of honor around the central image, I placed important facts about my four grandparents: their names, and birth, immigration, marriage, and death dates. My mother's name was Violet, so I used violet floss to embroider her mother's information—and by default, my dad's mother's data. For the grandfathers, I chose to use green floss. The grandmothers are at the top and bottom, the grandfathers are on the sides. Anna and Axel meet in the upper left corner with their daughter Violet in the adjacent light blue area; Anna and Charles meet in the lower right corner with their son Ewald in the adjoining light blue area.

The provinces have representative flowers, so I searched here and in Sweden for authentic patterns to add to the quilt. Ribbons trace the emigration routes from Sweden to America for each of the trips. I found photos of the ships the immigrants came on and embroidered them, each in scale with the others, together with the year and ship's name along the ribbons. There are three feeder ships in the North Sea and three transatlantic ships.

To complete the quilt top, I added a border that hangs down the sides of a bed, to represent a light blue sky, a medium blue ocean, and the deep blue sea. All the quilting is done to depict ocean waves. There's also a sleeve for a dowel rod at the top so it can be hung on a wall.

Done. I now have one quilt commemorating our ancestors, recording their emigration voyage to the new, bright, and promising land! Only one problem—one quilt, four children. They won't let me cut it into fourths, so you guessed it. One emigration quilt down and three to go!

—*Audrey N. Black, Ohio*

Appointment in Ghana

There is something magical about the air in Ghana. It is heavy with moisture from the Atlantic Ocean, fragrant with the smells of paprika and peppers, and thick with the scent of the roasted peanuts that are at the heart of so many Ghanaian dishes. But there is something else about the atmosphere—an eerie feeling that causes me to turn and look for someone standing beside me even when I know I am alone.

I don't find it disturbing. At least not anymore. Now I understand that I have been singled out by the spirits of my ancestors to tell their stories. It is their presence I feel beside me, and it is why they whisper incessantly from the moment I arrive in the country, "Where have you been, daughter? There is work to do."

I understand, with my first whiff of Ghanaian air, that absent any proof to the contrary, this is where my family's history begins. As an American descendant of slaves, I have few facts to go on when it comes to tracing my country of origin. Scant records were kept, and even fewer still exist that tell how my parents' people ended up on cotton plantations in Natchez and Vicksburg, Mississippi.

But statistically speaking, since historians believe that more than half of the approximately sixty most active African slave transport sites were in the Gold Coast area of what is now Ghana, there is a good chance that my ancestors are from here, or at least passed through en route to the Americas. That might explain why I feel so connected to Ghana.

"A lot of black people feel that way when they come here," says Hamet Maulana, Ph.D., a history professor at the University of Ghana. "I believe that there is a binding chemistry right down to our DNA that draws us here even five hundred years later." Maulana is one of a handful of African American expatriates who have relocated to Ghana. He doesn't appear a bit surprised, and is even a little amused, when I tell him that the spirits of my ancestors seem to move around me when I am here. "I know," he says with a smile. "As the Ghanaians say, 'You don't have to teach a child who her parents are; they will teach her themselves.'"

At their regular communing spot under a baobab tree at the W.E.B. DuBois Memorial Centre for Pan African Culture in the capital city of Accra, I am introduced to a group of African Americans who have settled in Ghana. I explain to them that I am preparing for a trip tomorrow to Ghana's notorious slave dungeons.

"Get ready," says C. K. Amoah, a dark-skinned man in his mid-fifties. "Sometimes the spirits there are very active." Amoah tells of a recent incident in which the remains of two former slaves were returned from their burial sites in North America to the Ghanaian dungeons as part of a repatriation ceremony.

He says—and swears it is true—that the two boxes containing the remains, no more than twelve inches long, suddenly became so heavy that when it came time to remove them from the canoe, eight grown men could not lift them. "The ancestors resisted mightily," Amoah says, "until we assured them that they were being returned through the dungeons this time, not being taken away."

My journey begins with a long bumpy drive over difficult roads to the small village of Asin-Manso, the last inhabited stopping point between the hinterland and the coast. It is also the place where, hundreds of years ago, captives had their last formal bath in Nan Kasuo or "Slave River" before the torturous overland journey to the slave holding quarters in the cities of Cape Coast and Elmina.

Asin-Manso is surrounded by a large stand of trees. Smoke curls upward from open cooking fires nearby. It is the beginning of the rainy season and everything is lush and green from a recent shower. The river's edge peeks out from behind the trees.

A woman, with her son of about ten, wants to sell me a clay urn that has just been removed from the kiln. "My son made it," she says, pointing out with pride the blue and white rivulets that decorate the sides. I ask her if she knows anything about the village of Asin-Manso.

"Many people died there when they were taken from their tribes," the woman says, inclining her head to the north. "They are buried over there." She points to a serene grove of trees near the river's edge. In fact, it's a mass grave, and to this day it is taboo to farm there or, she says with a look of warning, to even disturb the vegetation. I don't dare ask to be taken any closer. And I notice she does not offer to take me.

The drive from Asin-Manso takes about two hours, and I arrive at Cape Coast just as the sky becomes heavy with storm clouds. Rain pours down as I walk inside the outer archways leading to the castle and dungeon. How fitting, I think to myself, that the sky should cry.

The forts and castles built along Ghana's Atlantic coastline by Europeans beginning in the fifteenth century once stood guard against invaders who sought to raid the brisk commerce being conducted in gold and human flesh. Today they are monuments to Ghana's role as the center of the slave trade. This one in Cape Coast is easily the largest edifice in the area, and dwarfs the tiny fishing village that surrounds it. The castle is stately and imposing. Whitewashed and clean, it is dominated by a church located in its center.

The dungeons sprawl along the bottom of the castle, forming a network of tunnels and basement rooms. The ocean gathers and spills at the base. A plaque explains that the bottommost room is situated below sea level so troublesome slaves could be placed in it and drowned by the rising tide. The iron bars face the ocean; the victims could watch the deadly waves engulf them.

The dungeon just above the death chamber is labeled "male slaves" and is reached by feeling along the walls and descending a series of spiraling paths. Each turn shuts out more light and is blacker than the one before. I am joined in this journey into darkness by four other visitors: two European men; the Reverend Othelia Moody, a striking, six-foot-tall, black woman from Brooklyn, New York; and Stephanie Hazel, a Ghanaian woman. The two women are new friends and have joined hands to support each other through the frightening ordeal.

"I'm not sure I'm ready for this," says Moody. "It's not easy seeing this up close."

"It's okay," says Hazel. "I've been here before."

"Yeah," replies Moody, furrowing her brow. "But it makes me mad."

We wind down into one jet-black pit after another and when we reach an area lit by a single bare light bulb, John Andoh, a young docent, appears.

"You may be wondering," he begins, "why the floor of this dungeon level is slightly higher where you are standing than over here where I am. What you are standing on is eight inches of human waste and skin cells compacted over hundreds of years' time." It is difficult for me to resist the urge to leave now, and be sick.

"How many men were here?" someone asks.

"About three hundred at a time," says Andoh. "But five to six million slaves came through this port."

That would explain the growing sense of uneasiness I feel. I picture this dark, dank room full of men and boys; some tall and lean, others short and stocky, all drenched in sweat, filled with anger and despair. There is a sense that they are mortified at the descriptions we are hearing of their conditions, "... covered in feces, scabies, and lice," explains the docent. Yet I know that the men in this room would not want their suffering unchronicled. And so I stay and listen to every word.

Feeling our way back up, we cross the courtyard to the sign reading female slaves. The passageway leads to an underground dungeon big enough to hold perhaps fifty people. Here I scramble to find a tissue to cover my nose. The smell is ancient and acrid. The docent explains, almost clinically, how three hundred women were herded into this pit where they ate and slept in their own bodily wastes for up to three months. Moody, fishing in her purse for a tissue, shakes her head back and forth. "My God, it smells like they're still here," she says, her voice muffled behind the tissue.

I say nothing. But of course I know that they are. The presence of spirits is even stronger here than in the men's dungeon. I want to feel the stone floor underneath my feet; to feel what those women felt standing in this place. I step out of my sandals and feel the surface of the floor against the soles of my feet, then kneel and touch it with my hands. A child was delivered on this spot. A young girl died over there. A woman braided another's hair in this corner to pass the time. Over there a teenager wept for her mother. "We are in every crevice of this place," they seem to be saying. "Please don't recoil from us now."

I do my best to take in every detail so that I can understand the sheer terror, shame, and despair innocent girls and women must have shared in this room. On the way out, there is a staircase that leads directly to the living quarters of the fort's governor. He had, it is explained, his choice of the women.

It is at the "Door of No Return" that I understand with a rush of sadness exactly how I have come to be an African in America. Through this door, hundreds of years ago, a brown-skinned girl who looked just like me was marched from the dungeon and onto a waiting ship, bound for the Americas. There were no cameras to record this holocaust. Drawing word pictures may be the best I can ever do to depict the suffering and death of so many, as well as the triumph of spirit that enabled millions to survive.

I am filled with a profound feeling of pride and gratitude to be the descendant of ancestors who were able to survive entombment in these dungeons, the hell of the ocean's "middle passage," and the indignities of that "peculiar institution" called slavery.

When we emerge from the dungeons the skies have cleared, and the African sun forms a golden globe overhead. I reach down and scoop up a handful of Ghana's rich, deep red soil to bring home with me. If I don't see these shores again, I tell myself, this handful of home will remind me of the ancestors' requirement of me: "Tell them that you know of us," they say.

I give them my word.

—*Renée Kemp, California*

Photo by Peter Bregg, appeared in "The Search for Roots," in the September 20, 1999 issue of *Maclean's*. Used with permission.

Your Roots
Are Showing

Not with that tattoo!" As an actor, I've heard this comment more times than I care to recall, but I really don't mind. Just as casting directors sometimes use my tattoo to rule me out for a role (too much hassle to keep it hidden from the camera), I use my body art to help me sort out which assignments to accept. Experience has shown me that those who are willing to accommodate the tattoo of the rather conspicuous family history handiwork blazoned across my back make good bosses. If they're willing to tolerate or work around the tattoo, it means they truly believe I'm the man for the job.

What prompted me to become a living billboard for the LeGendre name? It was all triggered by an incident in math class when I was a teenager. My teacher enjoyed taking an occasional poke at his students. When I couldn't answer a question one day, he snorted, "I would expect more from a Legendre."

Clueless, I asked him what he meant. That was the first time I ever heard of Adrien-Marie Legendre, a French mathematician famous for his work on projectiles, ellipsoids, celestial mechanics, and other mysterious sounding topics. I later learned that his *Eléments de géométrie* was a leading text in the 1800s, but I was more interested to discover that he is commemorated on the Eiffel Tower and has streets in Paris and even a crater on the moon named after him.

All of this was news to me as I had never given my heritage any thought, but the possibility of a relationship to this mathematical genius was enough to spark my curiosity. I consulted a professional genealogist, whose comment on my surname made me all the more determined to find out about my family. The word LeGendre translates to "the in-law," and the researcher speculated that one of my ancestors had probably married into a wealthy family. Rather than allow the interloper to water down the family's reputation with an unknown surname, the qualifier "le gendre" was probably added to his wife's maiden name. Over time as the family's status faded, the bulky, combination surname was shortened to LeGendre.

I had to know more, so soon after my high school graduation, I began researching in the Canadian National Archives located in my hometown of Ottawa. Thanks to Catholic marriage records, I was able to trace the family back to the first French settlers in Montréal in the 1600s. Four hundred years later, I was raised bilingual in French and English.

Now it all made sense! I've always felt an attachment to France and French culture. During a school trip to Paris in

1985, I was reluctant to come "home" to Canada. I remember wanting to hide and stay behind because I felt so at home there. Finding my pure French roots explained my attraction to all things French.

Discovering my heritage shed light on other aspects of my personality too. My research revealed family traits such as the inability to hold a grudge and an overwhelming desire to do something noteworthy. Although I haven't conclusively proved the connection to Adrien-Marie Legendre yet, I continue to gather evidence. Adrien-Marie was known to have graciously dealt with rival mathematician Friedrich Gauss, who had a habit of occasionally taking credit for others' work, including Legendre's. I also believe that Adrien-Marie's mathematical endeavors may have been his means of making his mark.

When I was about twenty-two, I decided that I also needed to make a contribution. And what better way to show the world how proud I am of my family's legacy than by having emblems of our heritage tattooed on my body?

Inspired by some Scottish friends who had tattoos representing their clans on their arms, I decided to go them one better by having a large heraldic design etched across the top of my back, just below the collar line. The French embassy put me in touch with another professional genealogist who supplied me with an intricate design of stag antlers, stars, and chevrons said to be associated with the LeGendre name.

I approached a tattoo artist. His artwork required four painful sessions of five hours each, but my friends helped me through the ordeal by bringing me soda cans to crush and a mouthpiece to bite down on. All my friends aside from the Scottish ones thought I was crazy, but my mother's response was, "Good for you!" My grandmother told me how proud my grandfather would have been if he were still alive.

How do I feel about it six years later at the ripe old age of twenty-eight? Maybe it was a little drastic, but I don't regret it. I didn't do it for attention's sake and it might have cost me some acting jobs, but it helps me feel like I'm me and serves as a constant reminder to make a contribution. Every time I see it in the mirror, it's like an alarm clock reminding me of things I need to get done and shouldn't put off. For me, the decision to "let my roots show" was definitely the right one.

—*Erik LeGendre, Canada*

Photo copyright Caroline J. Jackson. Used with permission.

Beholden

Early in the morning of May 28, 1864, as the night was fading into dawn, Martha Jackson was awakened by the song of a mourning dove on her window sill. Its song was of horror and sadness; no tinge of joy or mirth was there. Martha Jackson realized, at that instant, that this was the Lord's way of telling her of the death of her beloved husband, Benjamin Franklin Jackson. She rose from her bed, dropped to her knees to pray, and wept softly, lest her grief be seen by her family and be considered impetuous and a product of superstition. She made a note of her revelation in the Holy Bible.

I wrote these words about a family legend that was handed down to me almost exactly a century after my great-grandmother's experience. Even today at eighty-seven and a half years of age, I visit Martha Matilda Stubbs Jackson's gravesite six times a year.

57

Down South, we have an expression we use quite frequently—beholden. Even though I never knew them, I have always felt beholden to my great-grandparents. In addition to my name, they left me a legacy of tradition, a form of living and belief that infuses every aspect of my life. It is a powerful force and an enormous blessing, but also a burden in the sense that I have always been aware of my obligation to reciprocate.

Raised as I was around three loving grandparents, family history has been a natural part of my everyday life since the days of my boyhood. The glaring exception to this was the Civil War, or as I was instructed to refer to it by a Confederate veteran who used to speak at my school each Decoration Day, the War between the States. For those who had lived it, the war was such a nightmare, such a tragedy, that they simply could not discuss it. Any and all questions from curious youngsters were summarily dodged or dismissed.

Even so, I heard from time to time from my father and his sister about a collection of letters still stored in the cloth bag Martha Jackson had used to contain them. I even saw the sack on occasion, but as the letters were all tightly bound with ribbon, I couldn't bear to unfold them. When I finally ventured to do so in the late 1930s, some seventy-five years after the war had ended, I was swept into a world far different from the romantic spectacle portrayed by the recently released *Gone with the Wind*.

Benjamin Franklin Jackson's happy marriage of less than two years was interrupted by the call to arms of the Confederate States. Leaving his wife and infant son, he joined the Army in June 1861. Over the ensuing three years of his service, he and assorted family members exchanged 125 letters. These letters, now fragile and musty after so many years, shocked and saddened me because they were so somber and emblematic of death and deprivation.

And yet the letters also reflected man's innate nobility. The everyday emotions and experiences of an ordinary foot soldier who is trying at once to fulfill his moral and religious ideals and his country's needs were evident on every page. In spite of intolerable hardships and premonitions of his early demise, for he closed almost every letter with "I am yours until death," my great-grandfather did his utmost to honorably discharge what he recognized as his obligations.

This remarkable collection had been passed down to my aunt who had four children of her own, but in the 1940s, she kindly entrusted me with the letters. She felt, as she told me, that I would "do the right thing."

Just married in 1941, I was busy with my own family life for several decades, but as the centennial of the Civil War approached, I finally found the opportunity to publish an anthology of these letters. I was delighted in April 1965 to be able in some small measure to reward my aunt's faith in me when I presented her with a copy of *So Mourns the Dove*.

In the course of compiling and editing the letters for publication, I also took it upon myself to write to the National Archives for a copy of my great-grandfather's service and pension records. When the packet arrived, I was left momentarily speechless when the papers confirmed that he had indeed died early in the morning on the exact day family legend held the mourning dove had sung so plaintively to my great-grandmother. I knew then what the title of the book would be, as its entirety is permeated by what happened at the last.

My great-grandparents left me with the double-edged gift of a legacy and the resultant responsibility to somehow repay this debt. I have ensured the posterity of their words and experience in *So Mourns the Dove*, and have tried to live according to the code of conduct they passed down through the intervening generations. I only hope I have acquitted myself adequately.

—*Alto Loftin Jackson, Alabama*

The UnWritten

Working with one photo at a time, this site will show you how to research, write, and save your photo-stories. A photo-story can be as simple as an informative caption, poem, or short story, or as complete as a biography. It can include portions of a diary, notes, or a log. By exploring the windows of your past, you will find some of the most exciting stories that are yet unwritten and gain a better understanding of who you are. As the The UnWritten team, our quest has only begun, yet it has already taken us back many decades through great adventures, horrid tragedies, ghost stories, and natural disasters which we share as examples.

We are Karisa and Charanna, two of the three authors and webmasters of The UnWritten, and the above is part of the introduction to our award-winning site. As fourth cousins descended from Benjamin R. Harrison and his second wife, Henrietta Simms Harrison, we had never known of each other, much less met each other, since we live far apart in Alaska and Minnesota. Given that Benjamin was born in 1826, it's a long way back to our blood connection, but thanks to the sleuthing of our third partner and cousin, Mandy, we found each other online and developed this site together long-distance.

Karisa: My first cousin, Mandy, had heard of ThinkQuest, a non-profit organization that offers programs to advance education through technology, from her mother. Every year, ThinkQuest holds a competition for student-designed websites, and Mandy thought we should give it a go. Through a little surfing, we found our distant cousin, Charanna, and invited her to join us.

Charanna: Mandy and Karissa already had a general idea of what they wanted the site to be before they found me. I was motivated from the start because I knew it would be a great opportunity, and I was really interested in the topic because my mom passed away when I was nine. I had so many photos, but no clue how to figure out who was in them. Through creating the website, I discovered a story for almost all of my mom's mystery photos!

Karisa: We communicated mostly through e-mails and each of us added our own touch to the website. I was in charge of editing and pulling stories together, as well as some java and other technical work. Char contributed other stories and research, and served as our spokesperson when we finally got to meet face to face in Switzerland for the ThinkQuest awards ceremony. Mandy did most of the programming and actual site-building. Whenever we got an idea about the layout, pictures, graphics, or anything else, we would send it to the others to see if everyone liked it.

Charanna: Mandy was our tech specialist, and I must say that she is a genius, especially when you consider that she was only thirteen years old at the time of the website's creation! And it's important to know that we made all of our decisions together. Nothing went into the website without everyone's approval.

Karisa: There has been nothing but positive response to our website. We've received messages from all around the world, from teenagers to college professors, and we've been very happy to hear how different, informative, and useful it is. There aren't a lot of websites like ours out there and people tell us that it will make you laugh, cry, and smile while you're learning.

Charanna: It's been a great experience for all of us, and I know that I've learned that team work is everything. It's also been very rewarding for me personally because I had never opened the journal my mother had kept from her late teens until a few weeks before she died, until I became a part of this team. It was only then that I realized what I had been missing for all those years because I hadn't opened her journals. I got to know who my mom was and that is powerful. Just maybe our website will result in some similar experiences for others.

—*Karisa Powers, age 15, Alaska and*
Charanna Smith, age 16, Minnesota

To learn more about The UnWritten, visit
<http://library.thinkquest.org/C001313/fmain1.htm>.

Scavenging for Ancestors

We were planning activities for a long weekend celebration of our parents' fiftieth wedding anniversary. Because we were bringing together both sides of the family and people of all ages, we wanted an activity that would serve as an icebreaker and allow all generations from all locales to have fun together. As genealogists, we also wanted to introduce everyone to some family history without boring them with charts and dates.

We found the perfect solution: The Great Stuever/Brennan Scavenger Hunt of 2001. Our photo scavenger hunt got people out to all parts of the community to sites that are meaningful to the family. Instead of gathering prescribed items, teams were required to take photos of their team doing something that showed some understanding of our ancestors.

Making the maps needed for the hunt was a good opportunity for us to track important places in our family's past—farms and homes, churches, schools, and more. Once we had marked about twenty-five sites on the map, we chose nine to include in the scavenger hunt.

We called ahead to ask the owners of certain places for permission to use their property for the hunt. We photocopied the maps and rules, and purchased disposable cameras.

The rules for our photo scavenger hunt were simple. Everyone on the team had to be involved in each picture, so if they weren't taking the photo, they had to be in it. Of course, each group needed a legal driver and a vehicle. Because of our concern for safe driving, we de-emphasized time and gave no award for being the first team to finish. They simply had to go to the right place and do whatever the instructions told them to do—as creatively as they could.

We let the teams determine the order in which they would visit the places. Although we had driven to the sites in advance to estimate how long it would take, we were surprised that every team made it to all nine sites in the two hours allotted.

Our photo-taking instructions were purposely vague. We wanted to make sure each team had enough latitude to get creative when it came time for their photo opportunities. Then we asked them to do some crazy things:

- Milk the concrete cow at the family farm.
- Conduct class outside the old Island School.
- Perform a cheer for Capac High by the old school bell.
- Form a human steeple at the Catholic church where our Irish ancestors were members.

- Act out the year of the Protestant Reformation, commemorated on the cornerstone of the family church where the honorees were married.
- Find a headstone bearing one of our surnames at a tiny, old country cemetery.
- Take a "family photo" with an ancestor whose portrait is displayed in the bank where he was president for many years.
- Demonstrate a farming method that could have been used on the original farmstead at the time of immigration.
- Prove that you've "got the beet" in a sugar beet field on the family farm.

Armed with a disposable camera, a detailed map and the cell phone number of someone who could help lost travelers get their bearings, the attendees split into five teams and went off in separate vehicles in search of family history. They were asked to turn in their cameras by noon. Lunch was waiting when they returned.

After we got the pictures from one-hour photo processing, the two of us left the party and acted as official judges. We gave teams points for photographing the right scene, involving all team members, and being the most creative. But since it was all for fun, we pretty much picked the funniest poses as the best. And there was no shortage of funny photos.

One assignment was to photograph the team acting out an old-time farming method on our great-great-grandparents' farm. Our aunts appeared in a hilarious picture. They claim they were cutting wood, we think they were hula dancing.

More than one team used tree branches as props as they reenacted a class session at the old country school. They used them as switches and sent students to the corner for punishment!

The matriarchs of the family—four sisters—did their own version of the scavenger hunt. They went to the sites that were most meaningful to them, then went wherever they wanted. Presumably the places were from their childhood and the owners didn't mind them posing on the front porch!

We gave the Goschka family a special award for putting up with our dad. Dad has lived his whole life in the Capac area, so he joined the out-of-town Goshkas to help their team navigate the map. After the photos were developed, we discovered that Dad had taken them to a completely wrong house. We felt lucky the owners didn't unleash the dogs on the strangers in their yard! Despite the blunder, Diane Goschka wrote to us later, "The scavenger hunt was one of the funnest events and got us out to see the community where the family grew up."

It was clear in the pictures that everyone had a good time. We posted all the pictures on bulletin boards for people to enjoy the rest of the weekend. Then we presented awards, giving each team some kind of a gag prize. The winning team was granted the right to be first in line for dinner. Later, everyone was invited to take home any photos they chose; we kept the negatives and index prints.

Our plan was to require teams to have at least one person from each of three generations on their team. But in all the excitement, people teamed up before we could say so. They were so excited about what was ahead, we just let them go! Teams ended up a little lopsided. One team had six people, while another had only three teenagers. It turns out that those details didn't seem to matter. No matter what the age or number of participants, each group had a great time. Better yet, their memories were captured on film forever.

—Anita Stuever and Sue Stuever Battel, Michigan

Photo copyright Steve Brosnahan, courtesy of Lower East Side Tenement Museum. Used with permission.

97 Orchard Street

I can still remember that harrowing day back in 1967 when my whole family moved to New York from Puerto Rico. The drive from our hometown of Moca to the airport had taken three hours, an eternity for a six-year-old, and then there was the plane ride. It was wintertime when we arrived and we were caught unprepared—no coats or blankets. I was so small and skinny that the snow covered me. I couldn't stop crying and I decided then and there that I hated New York.

Some forty years earlier, Rosario Baldizzi from Italy had a similar experience. Coming to America to join her husband, she had been full of anticipation, but was disappointed by what greeted her. The Lower East Side of Manhattan where they settled was dirty, treeless, and crowded. Had she really left sunny Palermo for this?

Although I spent all but the first six years of my life in the Lower East Side, my path was not to cross Rosario's until the late 1990s. An acquaintance came to me with an ad for a position in a museum and suggested that I apply since it was so close to where I lived. I wasn't looking, but I was curious. I never even knew there was a museum in my neighborhood!

Within short order, I got the job at the Lower East Side Tenement Museum located at 97 Orchard Street. From 1863 to 1935, more than seven thousand immigrants had lived at this address for at least a brief period of time. The museum's purpose is to celebrate the immigrant experience by bringing their stories to life.

By recreating to the tiniest detail the apartments of some of the actual families who had lived there, the museum lets visitors take a temporary trip into the world of the immigrant. In 1874, Nathalie Gumpertz, a German dressmaker, became the sole support for her four children after her husband mysteriously disappeared. The Rogarshevskys, an Orthodox Jewish family from Lithuania, lost their patriarch to tuberculosis in 1918. A decade later, Rosaria Baldizzi and her husband Adolfo moved in with their young son and daughter and toughed out the Great Depression until 1935, when the landlord closed the building rather than make mandated improvements.

I felt an instant connection to all those who had lived in this tenement, but the moment I stepped into the Baldizzi apartment, I almost fainted because it was so much like the one my family had when we first arrived. We had running water, but otherwise, everything was the same—the three, cramped rooms, the time-worn stove, the old-fashioned toilet. There was no heat or air conditioning; in fact, there wasn't even any ventilation. How tiny the apartment must have seemed to Rosario, just like our first apartment had felt when we squeezed nine people into it.

Like Rosario, I knew the feeling of being an immigrant. You don't know the language or the culture and you have no choice but to adjust and assimilate. It's true no matter where you come from or where you go. It's this personal experience that I try to bring to visitors whenever I lead tours of the Tenement Museum. Each time I step into the Baldizzi apartment and start to feel that emotional sensation of going back home, I try to take them on that journey with me.

Like millions of links in the immigration chain before us, Rosario and I both eventually moved past our first impression of New York and grew to consider this place home. But just as neither of us ever lost our accents (and I'm very proud of mine!), this nation of immigrants should never lose the knowledge of what it is to actually be an immigrant.

—*Georgina Acevedo, New York*

Photo courtesy of Lake View Cemetery. Used with permission.

Dinner With
the President

Who could turn down an invitation to dine with the president and his wife? Yes, it's true the event was to be held in a cemetery and that our host had been assassinated almost 120 years ago, but as we were to learn, he was as gracious as ever.

On 25 June 1998, President James A. Garfield and his wife, Lucretia, welcomed us for a memorable evening of chamber music, Dom Perignon, roses, caviar, and carriage rides. It was a soft, warm, summer evening and we were transported through Lake View Cemetery and time itself as we gazed up at the beautiful, old trees and listened to the clop, clop, clop of the horse's hooves on our way to the Garfield Memorial where the dinner was served. Even if the evening had been less magical, we could never forget the date because it also happened to be our forty-ninth wedding anniversary. And this was, after all, the very place we had become engaged.

Riding and dining with us were Bill Garrison, president of the Lake View Cemetery Association, and his wife. They introduced us not only to the "Garfields," look-alike actors who specialized in portraying the presidential couple, but also to direct descendants of both Garfield and McKinley, two of the seven presidents Ohio has given the United States. From Bill, we also learned how close we had come to receiving an invitation to spend the night with the President!

He explained that the cemetery had a long heritage of reclusiveness due to its efforts to protect against vandalism and disrespectful behavior, but now officials wanted to send a new message to encourage people to use the cemetery in an educational way. They learned that many locals didn't know Garfield was buried there, and if they did, they didn't know who he was or what he stood for. The cemetery association felt that a tribute to the President would help raise awareness of the historic aspect of the cemetery and commemorate the remarkable man himself, as he was, in a sense, one of our national ancestors.

As much as he wanted to draw attention to this proud history, Bill drew the line when consultants suggested an essay contest to spend a night with the President—in the crypt with a king-size bed brought from a five-star hotel. Instead, he came up with the more elegant alternative of the dinner we were now enjoying.

When we saw the contest announcement in the newspaper and noticed the date, it was a foregone conclusion that we would have to enter, so we drafted our essay, being careful to stay within the fifty-word limit. Among the more than 750 entries received, ours apparently made an impression:

It was the lake view and the city view which led us as art students to the top of the Garfield monument to become engaged. It would be magically elegant and coincidental to celebrate our actual 49th wedding anniversary on June 25th with President and Mrs. Garfield.

Even half a century later we find ourselves explaining this choice, but anyone actually visiting the site would understand instantly. With its commanding view of Lake Erie and Cleveland, it is easily one of the most beautiful settings for miles around.

And so it was very appropriate that we should find ourselves nibbling on dessert on the upper terrace of the monument, in fact the very spot where our engagement had taken place. It was an evening unsurpassed for its culinary, historic, and romantic aspects, and though it was a little strange to share our anniversary with a deceased president, the inevitable paparazzi, and even the *Today Show* audience, we wouldn't trade the experience for the world.

—*Ernest and Sally Horvath, Ohio*

Unknown Soldier

Arlington National Cemetery is a blustery place in November. Hundreds of rows of neatly aligned, memorial markers sprinkle the landscape as far as the eye can see, but there is little to prevent the wind from having its way with the living who venture among this ocean of white stones. Forewarned, I had donned long underwear under my black suit and winter coat, but I still found myself shivering as I attended the funeral of a man I had never known.

He wasn't my ancestor. In fact, I'm not related to him in any way. But as a so-called "Army brat," I felt privileged to have the unexpected honor of accepting the flag on behalf of his family. The head of the honor guard, usually so stoic, allowed a trace of emotion to pass across his face as he handed me the flag, and I knew that he was relieved someone was there to receive it.

How did I find myself in this peculiar situation? I'm a

researcher for the U.S. Army's Korean Repatriation project. In the years 1950–1953, thousands of American men died or went missing in Korea. Now, half a century later, U.S.-Korean relations are warming up. One consequence has been the return or "repatriation" of the remains of some of our anonymous soldiers.

Over the last five decades, the Army has lost track of the families of many of these soldiers. In most instances, the next of kin were parents who have since passed away. In other cases, they were siblings or wives who have moved, changed names, or are now deceased. Two generations have intervened and little has remained stagnant in our mobile, churning world. It is my job to find these families again.

When I succeed, the Army contacts the family and conducts mitochondrial DNA tests to positively identify the remains of the soldiers. When a match is made, the soldier can be laid to rest and his family can release itself from a fifty-year limbo of not knowing. Siblings, wives, children, cousins, and ever-so-rarely, an aged parent finally have a place to go to pay their respects to the loved one who gave his life for his country.

When I make the first contact with a soldier's family, the initial reaction is generally one of quiet disbelief. This is almost always followed by questions, cooperation, and even gratitude. It gives me tremendous pleasure to have some small role in bringing these soldiers home to their families. My father served in Vietnam and I had a dear cousin who was killed there. I can't say that I can put myself in the shoes of these startled family members when I cold call my way into their lives, but I'm familiar enough with their world to know that most of them are pleased to be found.

So I was rather surprised when I learned that the family of one of "my" soldiers was not coming to his funeral. The ceremony was scheduled, but only the priest and the honor guard would be there. Today's sophisticated technology was rendering the "unknown soldier" an antiquated concept, but in so doing, was revealing the almost sadder notion of the occasional "forgotten soldier."

It is understandable to some extent. In many cases, these soldiers have already been grieved twice—first, when they were listed as missing in action, and again when they were officially declared deceased. Perhaps it is just too painful to enter the mourning process a third time, half a century later. Preserved in their survivors' memories as heroic, young men, the very mention of these soldiers' names may well return people to a time of young widows and untapped potential. Maybe this explained the absence of this particular soldier's family on that gusty November day.

I suppose it was easier for me, a stranger who knew him only through documents and the voices of his relatives on the telephone, to attend his funeral. I only knew that his sacrifice needed to be acknowledged by someone, and so it was in the strange way life has, I found myself receiving the flag from the coffin of a man who had died ten years before I was born.

He is no longer unknown, and, at least as long as I live, this soldier will not be forgotten.

—*Megan Smolenyak Smolenyak, Virginia*

Following in
Their Tracks

It is night and it has been a hard day! The trail has given us a few problems today and we are all tired and ready to go to bed. We have only traveled a week, and already we've had trouble with the wheels on our wagon. Luckily, we were able to get to a wheelwright and have them fixed. We still have six weeks on the trail ahead of us so we feel better knowing that the wheels are in good repair. We had a steep trail today and the mules had to work extra hard to get our wagon to the summit, but they made it fine. Some of the walkers with the wagon train were at the top of the hill to cheer us on. The heat of the day settled on everyone, especially the animals, but we've had plenty of water. Yesterday, as we traveled through a rural community, we were greeted by hundreds of school children who lined the streets of the small town. Many were waving American flags to show their support.

As we settle for the night, my thoughts wander back a few years to the first time we joined a wagon train with my cousin in central Wyoming. It was 1995 and he was part of a wagon train traveling from Nebraska to Salt Lake City; he had invited us to go with him for a few days. We chose to meet him at Martin's Cove near Casper.

My great-grandmother, Ruth James, joined the Mormon Church in Wales and decided to leave her home and family to come to America by herself. In 1856, she had traveled this same route and was among those trapped by early, winter snowstorms during which many perished. She survived and finished the trip into the Salt Lake Valley, where she later met my great-grandfather, William Roach, who had immigrated from Wales four years earlier. They became the parents of ten children.

I wanted to retrace some of her steps in reverent respect for what she had done for me and my family. Sometimes my husband gives me the reins of our team and as I hold those reins in my hands and lift my eyes to the horizon to see where our trail is leading, I ponder whether she ever regretted her decision. Was she afraid? Did she wish she were back in Wales with her family? Did she question whether she would ever see them again? Did she at least have the comfort of Welsh traveling companions? I wonder.

After the inspiring experience of following in my great-grandmother's tracks, we joined other wagon trains commemorating the journeys of our pioneer ancestors. By the third trip, we realized we had wagon fever, so we bought a seasoned team of horses and purchased an old, coal wagon that we refurbished.

Now we travel with our children and grandchildren in the dated luxury of our own covered wagon!

We have learned that while living in a modern world full of gadgets and technology that tend to make us live at a faster pace, it is a welcome relief to get in a wagon, pulled by faithful mules or horses, join good friends, and travel at a much slower speed—four miles an hour! We have had good days and bad, short days and long. We have been thirsty and hungry, and have learned to appreciate the most basic of foods and a drink of water. We love to hear the sound of hooves as the horses plod along the graveled or paved roads, to hear the squeaks of the wagon bed, and to smell the sweat on the leather harnesses. Some days are exciting, some are ordinary, yet all are special. We appreciate a cool breeze on a hot day and the opportunity to have a shower. Many of the things we take for granted at home become very important—a good lantern as we go about our morning chores in the dark, ice to keep perishable foods from spoiling, and extra blankets to keep warm when the weather unexpectedly turns cold.

In contrast to the usual rush of our everyday lives, traveling four miles an hour gives a person time to think, re-evaluate, and focus on the things that are most important—enjoying a cold sandwich on a mountain ridge covered with scrub oak, seeing a jack rabbit dash through the brush, or admiring the strength of the mules as they take a steep grade. They are our heroes because they get us from camp to camp. It is a time to heighten appreciation for a blue sky, a lush valley of fields that produces food for a hungry nation, for life-giving water. It is also a time to give a silent, reverent "thank you" to my courageous ancestors who left homes, families, and businesses, spending weeks crossing the ocean on crowded ships, braving the unknown as they walked or rode across the plains, and finally conquered the Rocky Mountains and arrived in the Salt Lake Valley. This is what my ancestors did so that I could live in this great nation and enjoy the many blessings of freedom.

When joining up with a wagon, sometimes there are old friends among the travelers, but there are always a few you are meeting for the first time. Some have experience with wagons and horses, others do not. The first few days are awkward as conversations are brief and casual, but as the days wear on and troubles begin to make their appearance, it doesn't matter if a solid friendship has been formed. Everyone comes together to help whoever needs assistance, whether it be to replace a spare part on a harness, mend a wagon box, or share extra water. Before very long, there is a feeling of family and the resolve that we will all make our destination. As supplies, knowledge, and skills are shared, a feeling of brotherhood is evidenced each time people scurry to come to someone else's aid. There is no lumber yard or hardware store to run to; all we have is each other.

I guess that's the reality of a wagon train. We will lend a hand to others because we know that at some point in time, we will need their help, and we all know that we can depend on each other. That's what life is about—helping, sharing, learning from each other and developing a true love for one's fellow men— just like our ancestors did.

—*Shirlene R. Ottesen, Utah*

Home Swede Home

One of the high points of genealogical research is a trip to the birthplace of one's ancestors to see the original homestead, a visit usually commemorated with a photograph of the ancestral home. Unfortunately, that original homestead has often become a vacant lot, or the buildings have been so altered as to bear little relationship to their appearance in the era of one's ancestor's habitation. Faced with just such a situation, I have enjoyed the challenge of recreating my mother's original home and village in paintings.

On my first trip to Sweden in 1984, an elderly relative took us to see the site in northern Sweden where my mother's childhood home once stood in a village called Rödå. My first cousin, Nils, remembered visiting there as a small child. On a hillside overlooking the Vindelen River, he showed us the spot where our mutual grandparents had lived and our mothers had grown up. As is so typical, only a few broken bricks from the foundation remained. My photographic memento shows the two of us standing in a clearing in the woods looking at the rubble. At my request, Nils showed me a small house in the area similar to the one that had been torn down.

During my stay in Sweden, I learned about local architecture from my preservation-minded hosts, including the fact that the Västerbotten-style house evolved in this part of the country. Made of large, square logs, its low-ceilinged second story features small, decorative windows. Although unpainted in the early days, during the more prosperous 1900s, these houses were covered with wood siding and painted with traditional red iron paint.

Back home in Tacoma, Washington, I decided to recreate my mother's home in an oil painting, utilizing skills honed in painting and selling scenes of the Pacific Northwest. I compared the photos taken in Sweden with an amateur watercolor in my family since the 1930s. Although the young neighbor had tried her best to portray the house in Rödå as described, my mother was disappointed and never considered it a good representation of her native Swedish home.

Using notes from her journal written soon after she arrived in America in 1908, I planned a painting to show the house as it had existed. My mother, Matilda Johnsson, was born in Overrödå, Degerfors Parish, Västerbotten on 16 November 1881 to Kristina and Johan Peter Mattsson. Her story, written in Swedish, told how their first home had been lost in 1894 due to family illness. After they lived several years with her paternal grandfather, Matts Carlsson, her father inherited a little house in the neighboring village of Ytterödå, Umeå County. Mother described the house as "nothing stately, only an old grey, somewhat dilapidated building, but nevertheless so valuable to us who knew what it was like not to have a roof over our heads."

Using my photos of the site, the inaccurate watercolor, and my new knowledge of Swedish architecture, I brought my mother's homestead to life by painting a log *parstuga* (cottage) with a small barn, set among the ubiquitous birch trees and fronted by a typical slant-pole fence. The painting now has a place of honor in my home, and in 1996, it was selected by an art historian to be included in a curated exhibit of Swedish American paintings at Pacific Lutheran University.

Planning a second trip to Sweden in 1989, I hoped to locate my grandfather's original homestead since this was the birthplace of my mother. My wife wrote for assistance to the Regional Archives in Härnosänd. A researcher there found information on the tax lists about both this house and the adjacent home of Matts Carlsson, my great-grandfather. She then traced ownership of these properties forward into the 1930s. I also purchased detailed ordnance survey maps showing each plot of land, house, and other building presently existing. Armed with this new information, I hoped to learn who owned these houses now and thus find these two homesteads.

Once in Sweden, hospitable relatives drove us to the village of Rödå, chose a house in the proper vicinity, and knocked on the door. The family of Carl Mattsson greeted us. After discussion, it was decided that the house we were seeking would have been on the next lot, but had been torn down. With the help of a young relative who interpreted for us, we learned that this Carl Mattsson was also a descendant of my great-grandfather, Matts Carlsson. In fact, we soon discovered that this Mr.

Mattsson's aunt Teckla had lived with my parents in the United States for many years before returning to Sweden.

While we were talking, their son, Eric, arrived home from a trip to southern Sweden. He is the family historian and soon had charts spread out, tracing our relationship. He helped me photograph an ancient map of the area and generously gave me a book entitled *Et Sekel av Liv och Leverne I Rödå*, a recent historical effort by local senior citizens. Carl Mattsson took us outside and pointed out the land next door that had been Matts Carlsson's, land he had inherited and now farmed.

Upon returning home, I decided to paint the village of Rödå as it would have been in the 1890s when my ancestors lived there. An outline map in the book listed the owner of each house and even noted the year certain buildings had been moved and a new house constructed on the spot where Johan Peter Mattsson's house once stood. By studying the ordnance maps, comparing them with this outline, and using an old postcard showing a birds-eye view of the area, I painted the early landscape. Photographs I had taken during my visit were helpful in showing the general lay of the land. A few photos of unidentified Swedish houses in my mother's photograph album provided good details of the typical Västerbotten house and may have actually been the house in question.

We have shared photographs of these paintings with relatives, both in the United States and in Sweden. My cherished paintings of old Sweden provide an understanding of family origins through visual links with the past. This time, I hope my mother would have approved of the paintings.

—*Donald Olson, as told to*
Pamelia Schwannecke Olson, Washington

Photo copyright Perrin Todd Photography. Used with permission.

A Lucky Bloke

My first stage performance at age nine had nothing to do with my famous great-great-grandfather, Charles Dickens. As I strutted on stage in the magnificent rooster costume my father had concocted for my school's rather unconventional rendition of the Nativity play, I outshone the other stable animals by miles. People gasped, whispered, and laughed, and I reveled in their reactions. Preening and posing, I thought, "This is the life!"

When I became a professional actor, I deliberately avoided doing any of my ancestor's works. It's not that I had an aversion to his writing or that I had endured a tortuous childhood, being forced to absorb the family legacy by reading all his books. To the contrary, my parents never forced Dickens on us. My three siblings and I were allowed to discover him in our own time and our own way.

Photo copyright Will and Deni McIntyre. Used with permission.

And while we always knew we were related to him, our parents made it clear that this didn't make us special (although I confess that I was rather dazzled at age six to find myself sharing a pew with the Queen Mother at a ceremony commemorating the centennial of Dickens's death). Each of us, we were told, was to make our own impression on the world. Perhaps this is why I resisted performing his works, as I wanted to be judged on what I could do as an actor and not as the great-great-grandson of Charles Dickens.

But then came a request in 1993, the 150th anniversary of the publishing of *A Christmas Carol*, to give some dramatic readings from this well-loved story. Since the invitation came from the personnel director of the company my wife was working for at the time, it seemed prudent to accept in spite of my usual reluctance.

Pondering how to approach the performance, I thought it best to treat it as a script. It quickly became obvious that to make the story flow, I would have to develop a whole array of voices and facial expressions to convey the characters, particularly since there are twenty-six of them! I soon found myself spending hours practicing in front of a mirror.

At first, I regarded this as an interesting, one-time exercise, but I became more and more involved when I saw how the viewer was pulled right into the plot. I had feared that the audience would think I was being self-indulgent, but they were enraptured! I simply could not believe the power this had and I knew it was not my doing.

Obviously, there was a lot more behind all this than I had appreciated, so I began for the first time to research my noteworthy forebear in a serious way. I was both startled and delighted to learn about his own performing background and discovered that he, too, had stood in front of a mirror practicing expressions. I read the reviews from his second tour of America in 1867; they all remarked on his arresting eyes, animated face, impressive vocal range, and bold hand gestures.

I realized how theatrical his writings were and that they were intended to be larger than life. That's when I became Charles Dickens' number one fan.

So began my career of performing *A Christmas Carol* each holiday season in venues all across the United States. This story is stunningly easy to do because the characters jump off the page the second you read it. As much as I'd love to say that it's a huge struggle and it's my own brilliance on stage, the credit goes to the other Dickens because the characters are already there. They're living, breathing, and sometimes even misbehaving. And since everyone already knows the story, I can concentrate on the emotions and atmosphere. As soon as I began performing this classic tale, I understood what my dad meant when he told me, "Now remember, Dickens has done the work for you."

Perhaps my love of performing is in some sense inherited. Especially when I'm presenting *A Christmas Carol*, I am infused with an incredible amount of energy, which I assure you, isn't a feature of my everyday life. Something extra just comes from somewhere. I don't understand it, but I am content to let the mystery remain.

Now I travel constantly throughout the United States and United Kingdom to present the works of Dickens to as many people as possible. I'm not a literary scholar, so what's important to me is to portray the man. I want people to know what he was like—the energy he had, his sense of fun, and his grasp of tragedy. I like the old boy, you know?

Although I had sought for years to avoid comparisons with my great-great-grandfather, I now feel so fortunate, so proud, so privileged to be part of this family and to be able to do what I do. I am paid to indulge my hobby. Since that first performance in 1993, there has never been anything else. I can't imagine life without theater or the opportunity to represent my fascinating ancestor. What a fortunate accident of birth!

—*Gerald Charles Dickens, England*

Cemetery Saver

I don't think I fit the "cemetery saver" profile, if there is such a thing. It's not as if I'm going through life with a void that needs filling. I'm a thirty-three-year-old mother of a three-year-old boy. I work full-time and don't have a great deal of time to myself. I wasn't even born or raised in Lawrence, New York, so why have I launched the Lawrence Cemetery Restoration Project to save a pair of graveyards located there?

I stumbled into all this trying to find my great-grandparents' gravestones for my own family history, but it's also true that I've felt connected to Lawrence for as long as I can remember. My parents, both graduates of Lawrence High School's class of 1946, met on a blind date for the senior prom. They and my paternal grandparents (classes of 1919 and 1921, respectively) were wonderful storytellers. My grandfather, Glenford Pettit Craft, was born and raised in Lawrence. A cherished picture shows him

THE MOVERS, THE SHAKERS, THE HELPERS & THE RAKERS - LCRP 2001

learning to ride his bike there in 1907. In 1924, he and Nana eloped in a ceremony on the steps of Hempstead Town Hall. They later settled in a house on Court Avenue in what was called Sageville, a tightly spaced development of houses built by millionaire Russell Sage. Grandpa's father, Charles, was born in 1876, the year of the United States centennial. He was raised in Lawrence, just like the four generations before him, and all of them are buried at the Lawrence Cemetery.

Grandpa Craft used to come to stay with us every year during the holidays and regale us with his stories about the "old days." These tales were always about his old stomping grounds, the Five Towns—Lawrence, Cedarhurst, Inwood, Woodmere and Hewlett—and the beaches, cars, neighborhoods, and people that filled his life. It sounded like a Mayberry kind of place.

My maternal grandparents, immigrants from Hungary, owned Zila's Strudel Bakery on Central Avenue and another one on Irving Place & Broadway in Woodmere, both famous for their Russian coffee cake.

I may not live in Lawrence, but my roots are surely planted there.

My father and grandfather would grow a smile twice as big as their faces when they spoke about the old days and recently, I finally got a taste of why. I began to walk the streets and meet the people of the Five Towns. That's where the cemetery comes in.

About a year ago, I was surfing the Internet for genealogical tidbits and found myself visiting a Nassau County website with postings from people looking for family information. Noticing an old posting about the Lawrence Cemetery, I responded. From the reply, I learned that there are two separate yards to the Lawrence Cemetery, though I had only known of the one next to a Tudor-style church. Apparently, there was another yard hidden behind a large building. Having been bitten by the genealogical bug, I couldn't resist missing work the next day so my mother and I could drive back to her hometown to find this "newly discovered" cemetery.

What I found when we arrived was like a bad horror movie minus the zombies. The south yard next to the railroad tracks is a long, narrow piece of land. Luckily, I quickly found the family stone I was looking for right off the walking path, even though I hadn't the slightest clue of where it was. It's a huge stone and must weigh a ton. Fortunately, it was face up on the ground. On the stone were the names and dates I had been seeking. With all my ancestors gone, this was the only source that could provide this information for me. Many other family historians would not have been so lucky and would have found stones that are face down, making it impossible for them to obtain valuable data unless they should someday be lifted.

The cemetery looked like a truck had driven through it with graffiti and litter marking its evil path. There was mass destruction everywhere we looked. I thought to myself, "What kind of people mutilate and desecrate other people's gravestones?

These are people the vandals never knew, people whose families missed them terribly and still do in many cases."

As we drove away, I turned to my mother and said, "This is unacceptable. I have to write a letter or something. There's got to be something I can do." At that moment, I thought I was the only person in the world who was bothered by the decay and destruction. Little did I know that I was only one of an emerging tribe who had been there before experiencing the same feelings.

Within days, a reporter for the local newspaper called in response to the letter I had written. I was delighted, but did not have high expectations. The reporter asked a few questions and that, I thought, was that. But she took her investigation another step, apparently calling people in the local phone book who had the same surnames I had given her from some of the stones I had seen. One of her first calls was a direct hit. Ninety-year-old Virginia Hicks had spent her childhood Sunday afternoons planting flowers at her grandparents' graves in Lawrence Cemetery. Mrs. Hicks mentioned to the reporter that her cousin had a grandson, Scott, who had been interested in the cemetery for years. He, too, had stood there one day thinking he was the only person in the world who cared. Scott called me and we started to make a plan.

When the story ran several weeks later, I received only one phone call, but it was an important one from a woman named Jane Andrews. Her parents, grandparents, great-grandparents, and the generations before were all buried there. She had tried to do something about the cemetery about five years earlier, but no one was receptive at the time. Jane and I later learned that we are seventh cousins, giving us even more in common than our determination to rescue the cemetery!

It's amazing what can happen when a few seemingly lost souls with the same idea find each other, even when the scales are tipped against them. You never know what you are capable of until you try. A few of the seasoned locals told us that it had been tried before, but it had never happened and probably never would. Although we have had many moments of doubt, we refuse to let the voice of pessimism discourage us. Early this year, Jane, Scott, and I embarked on the new adventure without the help of any municipality.

So why would a woman who lives almost an hour's drive away try to rescue a cemetery that holds the remains of ancestors she never actually met? I'm convinced it's the spirit of my dad and Grandpa Craft. Grandpa wanted to be buried with his mother, Josephine Jackson Craft, who died at age forty-two, leaving her two sons and husband suddenly. He missed her until the day he passed away at eighty-four years of age, and always spoke of her as if he had seen her the day before. Sadly, in contrast to his wishes, he was not buried with her due to the condition of the cemetery. For this reason, I have dedicated this project to his memory and that of my great-grandparents.

In general, I am a hopeless optimist about our little army. We are not simply a few eccentric people with more time on our hands than we know what to do with. My innate belief is that people do care. Whether they actually act or not, they still care. And a project like ours gives people an opportunity to make a difference within the community. Every little bit does count, just like ants who must carry grains of sand one at a time to the top of the hill many times before it is complete. Whatever goodwill gesture can be made to help us, we will take it and continue to keep the faith.

It is my opinion that each of us can somehow find a little time to help someone or something somewhere. I think all of us could benefit from participating in an underdog project like this one; it challenges us, yet at the same time, gives our souls some much needed exercise. It is particularly satisfying to participate and progress in an endeavor that intertwines the blood of family with a spirit of dedication and giving. It gives me a connection to those whose stoic-faced, sepia-toned pictures I have stared at my whole life, and it makes me smile to think that they are looking down at me proudly.

—*Elyse Craft, New York*

Whispers of the Past

I grew up surrounded by the trappings of the Cold War and endowed with a rich and active imagination, so I just knew Grandma was a Communist spy. She had the foreign-sounding name of Judita Marcek Korbel and the heavy accent to go along with it. And all that whispering late at night, when she would sit deep in conversation with my mother and other women, was not in her usual, labored English, but in another language that sounded suspiciously like Russian!

Then there was her reticence. Having been a very curious little girl, I would occasionally quiz Grandma about her past, but she always changed the subject. All I managed to learn was that she was from a place called "the old country." I was only six at the time; not until the ripe old age of seven did I learn her "old country" was a place called Czechoslovakia. There wasn't much more I could do then, but I resolved that one day I would discover the

Judita Marcek Korbel

Photos from *Pictures from the Old Country*, a film by Susan Marcinkus, and was provided by the author and E.K. Waller Photography. Used with permission.

secrets of my grand-mother's past.

So perhaps it was inevitable that years later, as a filmmaker working on a project in Vienna, Austria, I would make a day-trip to nearby Bratislava, Czechoslovakia. It was the early 1980s, still a difficult time to travel in Communist Europe, so my first attempt to learn more only served to deepen my curiosity. Hearing everyone speak the same language I associated with the nighttime whispers of my childhood was tantalizing. I was closer, but still I knew so little.

During the so-called Velvet Revolution of 1989, Czechoslovakia freed itself from Soviet domination. I subsequently arranged to go to Bratislava to teach English at Comenius University. At that time, Czechoslovakia was undergoing the "Velvet Divorce" that would split the country into the Czech and Slovak Republics. Somehow it seemed appropriate that I should find myself in Slovakia searching for my identity at a time when the Slovak people were re-examining their own identity. Unfortunately, my excellent timing failed to bring any personal revelations, as I was unable to find my grandmother's village of Jahodniky Svaty Martin.

More determined than ever, I returned in 1999, this time with the intent of finding my family and filming the experience for posterity. I took on the role of detective. My sleuthing resulted in a meeting with a man whose father had worked in America and had sent home a wedding photo taken in Kenosha, Wisconsin, my hometown. The bride looked like my grandmother might have as a young woman, but it's so difficult to identify sepia faces edged in bridal regalia. I had never seen Grandma's wedding photo. Could it be her?

With the generous help of assorted archivists and genealogists, I finally succeeded in finding my grandmother's family. The camera crew captured every moment as my second cousins, daughters of the sisters my grandmother had left behind, greeted me with open arms and shots of *slivovitz*, the Slovak version of white lightning. Out came the old photos, including the same wedding pose taken in Kenosha, Wisconsin. So indeed it was my grandmother! How ironic and yet fitting that I should have to come to Slovakia to find this piece of my own not-so-distant past.

Through these new-found relatives, I learned that my grandmother's skill as a seamstress was her ticket to America. She emigrated alone in 1913 at the age of twenty-two, married, and raised four children. Her Slovak relatives imagined that she had led a comfortable life, much better than their own, but I knew better. Her husband lost both of his legs due to diabetes, so she struggled her entire life to take care of a family of six without the support and comfort of her extended family. And the construction of the Iron Curtain served to isolate her even from the occasional relief of a letter from one of her sisters.

My mother had a better life than what she would have had in Slovakia, and I certainly have a better life than I would have had in Slovakia, but it was Grandma who paved the way. While I decided at that moment not to correct my Slovak cousins' visions of my grandmother's life, I truly appreciated for the first time what an enormous debt I have to pay to the Communist spy of my youthful imaginings.

One day, I hope to bring my husband and son to Slovakia and possibly even buy some land and build a wooden house there. In the meantime, I'm doing my best to open the eyes of other Americans by sharing this experience in my film, *Pictures from The Old Country*. It may have taken half a lifetime, but I think I finally understand the meaning behind those whispers of the past.

—*Susan Marcinkus, California*

To learn more about Susan's film, Pictures from The Old Country, *e-mail her at zuza1 @aol.com.*

Road Trip

Afew years ago, my grandmother Grace and I sat on the couch turning the pages of an old album while Grandma related stories of the relatives whose images stared out from the black and white photographs. Then she pulled out some folded pages of lined notebook paper. "This is the journal your great-great-grandma Vic (Victoria Michael Penfold) kept on her covered wagon trip to Oswego, Kansas," she said. The journal was written in pencil on both sides of six small sheets. Here and there, the pages had been scotch taped and spots of water damage smudged the contents, but most of the precious pages were still legible. We sat for several hours transcribing the faded handwriting.

I realized that the coming summer, 1999, would be the hundredth anniversary of our ancestors' journey and I thought it would be a great adventure to retrace the migration route. So my

mother Lorine, niece Sara, nephew Dylan, and I decided to do just that. Dylan was initially disappointed when he realized we would be making the trip in a mini-van, rather than an actual covered wagon, but he was still game.

In preparation for our trip, I gave everyone an assignment. Dylan was to be our chief navigator. I sent him a copy of the diary and appropriate state maps from an old atlas so he and his dad could map out our route. We decided to fly to Kansas City and make our way via interstate highway to Milltown, South Dakota, where the diary begins.

My niece Sara was in charge of our finances, with a budget of $1,000. It was Sara's job each night to tally our receipts and keep us within our means. Her first shock came when I handed her the receipt for $300 for the mini-van before we even had our bags in the car! Sara was dismayed at how quickly we were going through "her" money, and it wasn't long before we stopped at a grocery store and were making our own peanut butter and jelly sandwiches.

It was Mom's job to read to us from the diary and old newspaper clippings along the way. In 1899, there were three generations of our family traveling together. Vic, who kept the diary, was thirty-seven years old and traveling with her husband, parents, children, niece, and nephew. One of her children, Altamay, would one day become my great-grandmother. All told, there were ten people traveling in two covered wagons in 1899. In 1999 there were four of us—once again representing three generations of our family—but this time with a few more modern conveniences to ease the way!

Our first stop was just outside of Kansas City at the National Frontier Trails Center in Independence, Missouri, where we saw authentic covered wagons and other artifacts that would have been a part of Vic's everyday life. One of our favorite exhibits was a wagon on a scale. We packed what we considered to be necessary items into the wagon and red lights would tell us when we had too much for the oxen to pull. This led to a serious debate on what to leave behind. The kids felt we could do without the coffee, but Mom and I vigorously disagreed!

On the second day of the trip, we made our way to the Henderson, South Dakota county seat to research land records and succeeded in finding documents pertaining to our family. From the courthouse we made our way over to the land that had once been theirs. Vic's husband Rufus proved-up his patent by planting cottonwood trees. One of the activities we enjoyed on our trip was picking out sights and items that were at least a hundred years old as these were places and objects our ancestors were likely to have also seen. We all posed for pictures and gathered up dirt from the family farm. We also picked up twigs from the cottonwood trees that we believed were the very ones great-great-Grandpa had planted.

It was at the Corn Palace Museum that we learned that South Dakota suffered a serious drought in the last decade of the previous century. This drought led to difficult times for area farmers and was likely the motivation behind our family's migration.

Each evening we wrote in our own travel journals, just as Vic had done. We found it interesting that in her diary she never once mentioned the fact that they were traveling by covered wagon, but then we realized that none of us had made any reference to the mini-van in our own journals. Vic did talk about the electric car in Sioux City. To her, that was a rare site!

Before our trip, I borrowed old newspapers on microfilm from Oswego, Kansas. The pages I had copied gave us a feel for the current events of a hundred years ago. We learned that the football boys didn't go to Oswego on Thanksgiving on account of a small pox scare and the telephone office at Labette was moved to the residence of D.W. Ream, where someone would be prepared to attend calls day or night. But it was the phone number for the newspaper's office, 69, that was most incomprehensible to kids accustomed to ten-digit numbers and cell phones.

At each site mentioned in Vic's diary, we stopped to take a photograph of something with the town's name on it and frequently picnicked in the local cemetery. We did this often enough that my nephew, who has the appetite of a professional football player, caught us off guard one day with the statement, "Look, there's a cemetery. I'm hungry." How could we refuse—even if the menu was still peanut butter and jelly sandwiches?

The original journal revealed that not every soul had survived that first trip, though it took us a while to sort out the details due to the scotch tape damage. Vic's entry for October 19th read, "Wednesday. crossed Boyer river came through crescent city & Honey creek. Lost Smart." Further reading made it clear that Smart was their dog. We were relieved to learn that he showed up again later along the trail, but were then saddened to read that soon after he got caught under the foot of a mule and didn't survive his injuries.

One of the stories my grandmother Grace remembers hearing was that Vic came down with cholera during the trip, though she made no mention of the illness in her journal. According to the family, when she thought she might not make it, she asked her husband, whom she called Mr. Penfold, to promise to take her back to her birthplace in Ohio to be buried. He could not honestly make this promise and told her he would have to bury her on the prairie. She is said to have retorted, "Well, then I won't die!"

On November 13th, she wrote, "Everybody Cranky. Come through Parson. Camped three miles from LaBettes City." The next day was the final entry in Vic's journal: "Got to Oswego this afternoon. Don't know how long we will stay."

When we arrived in Oswego one hundred years after the journal was written, we easily found the local historical society's museum right on the main street. We strolled in wearing commemorative t-shirts listing the people who made the 1899 trip, the cities they had passed through, and the names of the four of us who were retracing their steps in 1999. Our adventure was quite a hit with the folks at the museum. Having heard of our budget and regular diet of peanut butter and jelly, the museum kindly and wisely presented Sara with a complimentary copy of their publication *A History of Oswego*.

We thoroughly enjoyed our quest and believe we created special lifetime memories for the next generation. Upon our return, we created a scrapbook along with a shadowbox containing a copy of the land patent, a test-tube of dirt from the farm, and the cottonwood twigs. We also presented a program at our local genealogical society and brought—you guessed it—peanut butter and jelly sandwiches as refreshments. But we really knew that the expedition had been a true success when Sara told her grandmother that she would get As in social studies because, "Now I know that history is real!"

—*Jenniffer Hudson, Texas*

Paj ntaub by Xai Vong. Used with permission.

The Fabric of Our Lives

It is a curious feature of the American immigrant experience that those who come to the United States have usually been so consumed by the assimilation process that they rarely share much about their pre-U.S. lives with their children. This is unfortunate as these immigrants have rich histories often neglected and later forgotten. As an English as a Second Language teacher, I have had the opportunity to slightly alter this pattern for two classes of children, using a non-American tradition as the means.

Twice now, I have witnessed the flurried excitement generated among my students by *paj ntaub* (Hmong story cloth) projects. The impetus came from a poignant story, "The Flower Cloth," from a collection entitled *Tales of Courage, Tales of Dreams*

by John Mundahl. In this melancholy tale, a Thai grandmother refuses to leave the refugee camp as her entire clan leaves for America. She wants to die in her country, weaving all the sorrow of her life, color by color, thread by thread, into an intricate cloth diary. I thought it would be an eye-opening experience for my students to create story cloths about their mothers' lives.

My first experience was working on a three-week project with Hmong fifth graders whose families all hailed from Laos in an inner-city school in St. Paul, Minnesota. My second experience was with a multi-ethnic middle school in the same city.

In the first case we used the traditional, muted blue cotton background, carefully hemmed so the stitching did not show. Borders were selected from a Hmong folktale book entitled *Nine in One, Grr Grr!* by Blia Xiong. The border of tiny, white triangles, representing the mountains of Laos, was the most popular. Other borders such as circular patterns representing snails, for example, were usually not selected because of their complexity. Colorful shapes of felt, depicting the story line of their mothers' lives, were attached with glue to the blue background and allowed to dry. The bright winter colors were complemented with sequins for coins on the mothers' wedding dresses and with real feathers for chickens in the farm scenes. These ornate, 3-D touches represented the Americanization of the Hmong idea of the story cloth, which is traditionally a two-dimensional, totally embroidered work. The students, of course, had been Americanized in their transition from Laotian to American culture.

Prior to the beginning of the artistic venture, the fifth graders, all of whom were Hmong, were asked about prior knowledge of the Vietnam War and their mothers' escape from the war. Hazy bits of information were offered in response, but it was clear that there had been sparse communication on this topic. We talked about the importance of "knowing your roots" and realizing the sacrifices their mothers made on the long journey to freedom. We brainstormed questions they might ask their mothers about their childhood, youth, marriage, the war, the escape to Thailand, and their flight to America. Sample questions were typed and sent home to help the students interview their mothers.

The stories they came back with showed that communication had indeed taken place, and that the sensitive and painful topic of the war had been unearthed. Stories were edited and typed. Then the students drew a rough sketch of how their story cloth might evolve on a regular, white sheet of paper. Larger paper patterns were then made of objects in the sketch so they could be traced onto felt.

It was interesting to note that no two story cloths were exactly alike. But in general, the boys conjured up guns, fire bombs, and bodies in the river, while the girls used great detail to create the tranquil farm scene with their mothers feeding pigs and chickens, and constructed the beautiful wedding dresses worn by their mothers.

A typical paj ntaub featured an idyllic farm scene in the top left corner and the mother in her wedding gown in the top right, the flowing Mekong River with rescue craft dominating the mid-section, and an airplane in the lower left section, zooming to a small U.S. map in the lower right. Thus, the story was told in kind of a criss-cross fashion similar to the traditional paj ntaub.

As the project neared completion, I could sense pride of ownership growing strong along with their minds' innate desire to create pattern and meaning out of life. Finally, the students designed their own invitations to our "Mother's Tea." The culmination of our project was this wonderful event with tea, lemonade, and cookies. Mothers and family members were seated on chairs in the audience, while each student came up to the front and read their mother's story near their paj ntaub.

I will never forget the moment when one girl got up to speak and eyed her mother in the front row. Pointing to her cloth as she read the story of her mother's heroic escape for a better life, she looked lovingly at her mother. Finally, she spoke this sentence in conclusion: "You are a great and wonderful mother."

Tears welled up in her mother's eyes as she silently accepted this beautiful pronouncement. That touching moment said it all. All of the three weeks of hard work in art and writing were consolidated in meaning—a connection, a bond, a love between daughter and mother. The goal of honoring our mothers had been achieved!

My second experience with the story cloth project was equally amazing! It not only made connections between mothers and their children, but it also bonded the children of many countries as they expressed survival and transitions using the traditional Hmong story cloth idea. After discussing the "Flower Cloth" tale, my multi-ethnic class of Hmong, Ethiopian, and Mexican students was asked to create story cloths of their mothers' lives, including, if applicable, the survival of the Vietnam War and the arrival in the United States. This, of course, posed a problem for Jorge and Gustavo, my students from Mexico. Their mothers had not survived a war, but they had arrived in the U.S. from a foreign country. Ramadhan from Ethiopia could identify more with the process because her mother and the family had escaped a war in Ethiopia. While discussing the cloths, she explained, "We're all the same because we've all seen war."

Once again, when I asked the students about the Vietnam War, they knew very little. In fact, they knew even less than the students who had done the earlier story cloths. When the students read their oral reports about their mothers' lives to the class, it was easy to see that previously unknown information had been revealed. One of my students, Neng, was shocked to discover that he had a brother, five years older, who had died in Vietnam. In this way, the project helped the students learn more about their families.

Art materials this time included gold beaded wire, raffia for houses, yarn, deep blue satin ribbon for the river, and multi-colored feathers and shapes. These modern touches furthered the unstated message that cultural concepts change slightly in a new setting, just as the students' mothers had to change to adapt to a new life in America.

The thrill of awakening their minds through visualization of a story was almost as rewarding as seeing the bond grow between mother and child. These students honored their parents and ancestors by investigating their past, and I hope, will be a little better equipped to pass on their proud history to their own children.

—*Jeanette Stohlmann, Minnesota*

111

Homesteading in the New Millennium

Until a few years ago, I did my best to avoid my father's long family history lectures. Now my eighty-year-old father, Samuel Snipes, has found a fresh convert in me. Everything changed when I was introduced to what Dad calls a "sentimental collection of stones."

Three hundred and sixteen years ago, our ancestor Samuel Burges emigrated from England to Bucks County, Pennsylvania, where he bought farmland from William Penn. A Quaker farmer, he erected a home that was simple in design, but grand in scale by the standards of the day. About a century later, his descendants rebuilt the house. Ten generations later, I'm making plans to reclaim the reconstructed homestead, which had slipped out of our family's hands and deteriorated almost past the point of rescue.

Remarkably, generation after generation of our family continued to work the same land and attend worship at the same Quaker meetinghouse. They also maintained the old farmhouse—that is, until 1948 when some cousins leaving the area opted to sell the property. In 1970, it was resold to Falls Township to be used as a police station. An election resulted in a change of local officials and the plan was never pursued. Focused on a variety of other restoration projects, the township regrettably allowed the Burges structure to decline.

Slightly over two years ago, I started looking for a place to live. My brother-in-law, who has his own contracting company, suggested that I consider the original homestead. Though I grew up just down the road from it, I had never done more than stroll around it once or twice. But something about the notion appealed to me now. I explored the property and found it to be a decaying hulk. Still, I was captivated. I began having sleepless nights and sketching out how the rooms might look after restoration. Friends accused me of having been possessed by my ancestors!

For the first time, I became interested in the family history my father had tried to pass on to me. Exploring previously ignored attics and basements, I found letters dating back to the late 1700s. In one letter written by an ancestor in the 1860s, I noticed that she closed with "give my love to inquiring friends," an expression my mother still uses today. I found photos of the house taken in 1907 and of the relatives who had lived there— and evidence of the lives of people who had only been known to me as names on tombstones.

And I learned of family legends. Hannah, an African American housekeeper, was employed by my great-great-grand-

father. When one of his daughters was jilted by a local farmer, Hannah was said to have exclaimed, "Henry Comfort, I put a curse on thee! May thee never have a live child!" The farmer had married three times, but all his children were stillborn. I didn't think much of the tale until a distant relative shared a photo of an African American woman. On the back, someone had written, "Hannah Clark, died May 24th 1893, buried in Yardley, PA." Research on Henry Comfort revealed that he did indeed have three wives, but left no survivors. Hannah wasn't a blood relative, but she raised my great-grandmother. I went to the cemetery to pay my respects, grateful that the family lore had survived for over a century and amazed at the connection I felt to this woman. Like many of my ancestors, she had come alive to me.

I was addicted. I contacted older relatives and wrote down as much as possible. My sister and I began to film interviews. I paid more attention to the knickknacks stored away in cabinets and drawers and learned that objects have power. It's about who you are and where you come from. They give you a feeling of roots.

Convinced beyond any doubt that I must restore the old family homestead, I attended an estate auction of one of my mother's cousins to find authentic items to help furnish the house upon completion. Sickened to find family books, journals, photos, and letters for sale, I even went as far as to circulate among the crowd asking the others not to outbid me. Fortunately, many honored my request.

With the blessing of my family members, I arranged a property swap with Falls Township, which owned the family homestead. Since my family still farmed the sixty-eight acres next to the old home, we were able to exchange a piece of that land for the house and two-and-a-half acres around it. All of my siblings agreed to sign away their share of the family land that was being traded. All told, it took two years and three months to arrange the deed swap, but the whole family agrees that it was well worth it.

Now the hard work begins. With the help of my brother-in-law and other enthusiastic relatives, the restoration will start shortly. I intend to create a livable house (not a museum) but will try to be as true to the original design as possible. With Bucks County being the fastest growing one in Pennsylvania and the last of the old farms being sold for housing developments, there are few jewels left. It's more important than ever to preserve this piece of the past. This restoration is a spiritual endeavor that will be of service to the community as a whole. Once completed, I'll let the local historical society use the house for fundraisers and might even develop a demonstration farm that people could visit to temporarily step into the past.

An earlier generation may have let the homestead pass out of family hands, but I'll do my part to make sure that never happens to my "sentimental collection of stones." Once I move in, I'm there for life.

—*Jonathan Snipes, Pennsylvania*

Remembering Nona

Usually, when we speak of ancestors, we're referring to people who lived decades and maybe even centuries ago. And usually, when we plan family reunions, we gather the descendants of folks who lived generations ago. So I guess I was sort of breaking the rules when I recently held a reunion centered on my sister, Nona, who died only thirty years ago.

Nona passed away at the age of thirty-eight, leaving behind a husband and three children. Tragically, her only son died a couple of years later at the age of twenty-two. Due to unfortunate circumstances, Nona's daughters, Jeni and Cindy, rarely had contact with her side of the family over the ensuing years.

Her passing was especially difficult for me and my brother, Ben, as Nona was our primary care giver while we were growing up. While our mother worked to support us, Nona tended to us to the point of staying home from school when one of us was ill. Though the years passed, Ben, my mother, and I never ceased to mention her—somehow, someway—in any conversation we would have. It was not intentional or planned, but just a natural thing for us. And talking about Nona never depressed us; it just made us feel good to chat about memories that were as fresh as the day they were made.

About a year ago, I realized that it was almost thirty years since Nona's death. I thought with sadness about how her children and grandchildren had never really had the chance to get to know the wonderful woman I had known. The seed of an idea began to grow.

I pondered whether I might be able to find some folks who knew Nona. Fourteen years her junior, I hadn't known many of her friends, but my brother remembered quite a few. With Ben's help, I used my genealogical skills to track down assorted friends and relatives of Nona. Together, we organized a reunion to celebrate her life and share our memories with her daughters and grandchildren.

On the designated day, we had an outdoor picnic, played games, visited among ourselves, shared many hugs, and caught up on all our lives. Then came the time to share memories. Everyone grabbed chairs and found just the right spot to sit in our circle. I started by reminding everyone of the purpose for our gathering and Ben got the ball rolling by talking about Nona's loyalty and great sense of humor, including all the tricks she used to love to play on us.

One by one, memories emerged that seemed small on the surface, but held special meaning for the teller. For instance, Ben shared his recollection of the day Nona came home with a new car and told him he could use it. She had offered to let him—a sixteen-year-old boy—use her brand new car. What could be better? But Ben realized that trust was important and he never abused it. Nona's simple act of generosity taught him a lesson that stays with him still.

Those of us who knew Nona reminisced about how she used to play telephone gags on all of us. I reminisced about the days she would take me to the plays at the Cherry County Playhouse. And those who had never really had the chance to get to know her asked questions that the rest of us were delighted to answer, although it is amazing the questions that young people in their teens and twenties can think of.

Her children and grandchildren learned that Nona had tried her best during her years of illness to teach them self-sufficiency because she knew she would not be with them long. She was always loving and kind, but she would teach them practical skills or send them off to play, trying to keep them from becoming too dependent on her since she would not be there as they grew older.

Everyone shared tears and laughter, as we knew would happen—tears of sadness that she was not here with us and many more tears of happiness for all the wonderful memories she left us in such a short time.

I was thrilled to have a way to honor my big sister, but was even more delighted when I heard the reactions of her daughters. Said Cindy, "It was the best day of my life! I've never felt so close to my mom and her side of the family. It was really special to learn that I have a lot of her in me, that we do things alike that I was never aware of, even though I was so young when she died. I love that."

Jeni echoed her sister's thoughts, saying, "I loved being with my family again. From the stories you and Uncle Ben tell, it confirms that Mom was a kind and caring person, as I remember her."

Cindy and Jeni's husbands were also thankful for the insight they gained, claiming the experience helped them understand their wives' quirks better! In fact, everyone agreed that the reunion was so successful that we decided to do it every year.

It makes my throat tighten up just writing these words as I will always miss Nona tremendously, but I felt so happy and warm inside bringing her family together again and reminding them just how special she was. The day may have ended, but the memories will last forever.

—*Brenda K. Wolfgram Moore, Michigan*

Living Dolls

Inever intended to create a shrine for my ancestors, but that's exactly what my family calls my living and family rooms. These rooms are home to the twenty-six porcelain dolls I have created that represent members of my immediate family and ancestors going back five generations.

I chose a "when I grow up" theme for the collection, so all the dolls are children dressed in costumes depicting the life's work, a favorite hobby, or something unique about the person they represent. I aim to portray the essence, more than the exact image, of my ancestors. When I make a doll, I pose it with a photo of that person. The hair or eye color might not be the same, since I can't always be sure from old black and white photographs, but I try to capture a characteristic look or expression.

Each doll is displayed in a little scene including antiques or accessories that were used by the individuals or are representative of the period in which they lived. In making each doll, I take everything I know about the person's life and try to incorporate it, crystallizing it into a tableau. This is my effort to make them human to me—real people, family—not merely names on a chart or in an old family Bible. Because I live so far from my childhood home in Nebraska, this also gives me a way to share my family with my five children who never had the opportunity to know them as I did growing up, hearing stories at reunions, and seeing old pictures in albums.

Since I have never considered myself to be an artist possessing the necessary skills, it took a pretty critical time in my life to begin this hobby. I have always loved beautiful, porcelain dolls found at doll shows and fine collectibles stores. But I always suffered from sticker shock when I saw their price tags! The only way I would be able to afford one, I used to joke with my husband, was if I made one myself. We'd laugh and toss the idea aside.

Then my husband became seriously ill and required a liver transplant. We waited nine long months until a suitable liver became available and my husband's placement on the national list was high enough.

During that stressful time, I felt I needed therapy, but I could not afford to go to a psychologist. I decided that a creative endeavor of some sort would keep my fingers busy and my mind occupied. It occurred to me that learning how to make porcelain dolls would be therapy I could afford, so I began taking classes at a local doll store in the evenings and during vacations.

Though I was initially nervous that I might break something, I thoroughly enjoyed the experience. My teachers would not let me go home with an ugly doll and they patiently helped me. I

121

would dream about how to dress it and what color hair and eyes to put on it. In time, the doll grew into a little person for me.

The project has taken about seven years and has been an evolution, rather than the result of a full-blown vision from the start. I found that making dolls became addictive. I would finish one, only to find myself hungering to make another.

One night, I dreamed about making a doll that would look like my dad dressed in a sailor suit, because he served in World War II in the Navy for six years. At a yard sale, I found a model destroyer ship, and later my dad gave me an aftershave bottle in the shape of a mail carrier's jeep like the one he drove for the postal service until his retirement. His tableau came together perfectly.

Then I wanted to make a doll for my McNeal grandfather, a homesteader in Nebraska, who came from a long line of farmers. When I displayed his doll, I bought a miniature windmill from one of my visits back to Nebraska and a miniature John Deere tractor and plow like the one my grandfather used in his fields. I stacked miniature bales of hay and completed the setting with a wide-brimmed, straw hat and a handkerchief to wipe his brow.

My maternal grandfather worked for the Union Pacific Railroad for fifty years—he lied about his age when he was hired at the age of sixteen. So he is posed sitting in the middle of a model train set, wearing a striped pair of bib overalls and a conductor's hat with insignia. I didn't settle for toys, but instead used a scale model of a Union Pacific train set. He also played the violin, so I obtained a model violin that his doll plays during the Christmas season, just as I remember him doing years ago in our home after I had gone to bed.

There are stories for every doll I make and a photograph to go with it. I have even displayed my collection at my school and at two family history conferences. When I am asked which is my favorite, I always say my Sioux Indian great-great-grandmother. She was born on a reservation in Illinois, where she met my great-great-grandfather, a poor minister. When he asked her sister to marry him, she rejected him, and Amanda piped up, "Then I'll take him." They were married, had nine children, and later homesteaded in Nebraska.

The McNeals, I imagine, originally came from Scotland or Ireland where many Scots emigrated, but I can't prove it yet. My genealogy is stuck in 1802 in New Hampshire, so the doll I dream of dressing in a kilt made of the McNeal plaid and playing bagpipes goes unmade for the moment, but I'm sure he'll join the rest of the family someday.

—*Sheryl Sullivan, Utah*

The Long Gray Line

Webster's Dictionary defines ancestors as "predecessors, those who go before." Those who go before as graduates of the United States Military Academy at West Point, New York, are members of what is proudly known as The Long Gray Line.

In 1965, Lieutenant Colonel David Quinn, retired from the U.S. Army, decided that something special should be done to mark the hundredth anniversary of his father's graduation from West Point in 1866. Lieutenant Colonel Quinn received permission and official sanction from the Superintendent of West Point and then accepted the challenge of locating and contacting descendants of the forty-one graduates in the Class of 1866. On the first Monday in May 1966, over 125 descendants attended the first centennial celebration. The event provided descendants an opportunity to meet each other, tour the Academy, and attend a memorial service and parade by the Corps of Cadets in their honor.

This special occasion was intended to be a one-time affair, but word spread quickly and graduates of the Academy overwhelmingly thought that the event should be continued. A Permanent

Committee of searchers was formed. Over the years, many individuals have participated on this committee. The Permanent Committee is presently composed of four volunteers, three of whom are West Point graduates. Brigadier General Michael J. L. Greene, USMA 1941, heads the committee.

As a family historian and 1968 West Point graduate, I was thrilled to join the committee in 1991, viewing it as a great way to use my genealogical skills as a way of paying tribute to my alma mater. For the Permanent Committee, our most important, fascinating, and sometimes frustrating task is the research, letter writing, Internet surfing, telephone calls, and other detective work necessary to locate as many living descendants as possible of the men who joined the Long Gray Line, West Point's alumni, one hundred years earlier.

We start with an alumni file that has been maintained by the West Point Archives. As might be expected, these files are sometimes rich in leads, and disappointingly sparse at other times. Fortunately, we usually locate descendants, direct or collateral, for at least seventy percent of the graduates.

Regardless of how challenging our searches may be, we find immense joy in seeing our guests, ranging over the years from one hundred to more than two hundred, join us at West Point for a day of honoring their ancestors. In some instances, relatives meet other relatives they never knew or have not seen in years. In other instances, guests do not even know their ancestor had attended West Point. Still others have never before visited West Point, one of the treasures of our nation.

In support of this event, the West Point Archives staff provides descendants the opportunity to view their ancestor's academic and demerit records. Guests take great delight in reading of their ancestor's demerits for "dust under bed" and other infractions that are often later overshadowed by their ancestor's successful military and political contributions. A Last Roll Call ceremony, held in the Old Cadet Chapel within the West Point Cemetery, memorializes the graduates with a reading of the class roster and guests standing when their ancestor's name is called. This roll call, accompanied by a stirring rendition of "Taps," is a truly meaningful and moving event.

To my great surprise, in searching for descendants of William Tidball, USMA 1901, I located his first cousin once removed, and determined that I, too, was related to William Tidball—as a half ninth cousin! Of course, that meant I had now located a previously unknown half ninth cousin once removed! The final event of the centennial celebration occurs in the evening following a banquet. One descendant of each represented graduate speaks for three to five minutes about his or her ancestor. Needless to say, I deferred to my newfound cousin since his relationship was so much closer.

Classes from 1866 to 1902 ranged in number from thirty-seven to seventy-seven. These graduates of West Point have included names well-known to students of military history: Frederick Dent Grant, Charles Totten, James Franklin Bell, George Washington Goethals, Henry Clay Hodges, Jr., John Joseph Pershing, Charles Pelot Summerall, and Fox Conner. Some graduates have earned the Medal of Honor and rankings of General, while other graduates have served their country in various political and business roles. Regardless of the ancestor's activities and accomplishments, however, all those who attend these centennial events are all rightly proud of their ancestor and his part in history and in their heritage.

126

The Class of 1902 Centennial Celebration, the thirty-seventh continuous celebration, is particularly special as the year 2002 also represents the bicentennial of the founding of West Point on 16 March 1802. The Long Gray Line keeps getting longer— and I envision the day my own descendants will celebrate my place in the line in 2068.

—*Dale W. Hansen, USMA 1968, New York*

Photograph copyright Mimi Levine. Used with permission.

The Tower of Life

In the summer of 1979, I was on a plane to Russia, midway through a fact-finding mission focused on Eastern Europe. As a member of President Carter's Holocaust Commission, which was charged with making a recommendation for a suitable United States memorial to the Holocaust, I had traveled to a number of the "capitals" of the Holocaust Kingdom (including Treblinka, Auschwitz-Birkenau, and Plaszow) and was now on my way from Warsaw to Kiev. For days, I had been wrestling with the question of how to commemorate the people and the culture that had been destroyed.

Flying through the clouds, I suddenly realized that somewhere beneath me, just south of Vilna was the town of Eishyshok (Polish: Ejszyszki; Lithuanian: Eišiskes), where I had spent the early years of my childhood, before the Holocaust brought that peaceful idyll to an end. For a few happy moments

I allowed my imagination to return to those scenes of my child-hood, to wander from the beautiful synagogue to the bustling market square where my grandmother's drugstore and photography studio were located, from the Hebrew school that my brother attended and to the deep forests where I'd walked with my parents.

And then I knew what had to be done. Any memorial that aspired to do justice to the millions of Jews murdered in the Holocaust would have to go beyond documenting the horror of their deaths; ideally it would also memorialize their way of life, recreate it in all its richness and beauty. There and then on the plane, I decided that, whatever the recommendations of the rest of the people on the Commission, my own focus would be on painting a portrait not of loss, but of life before loss. I would do so by using my own beloved *shtetl*, since it was among the oldest ones, having been established in 1065, and was so typical of the thousands of small Jewish settlements that dotted the countrysides of Eastern Europe where two thirds of European Jews resided.

Eishyshok was established by a Lithuanian military prince, members of the army, and five Jewish families who came from Babylonia—among them the Azrieli, Ben-Asher, and Ben-Yossef, my paternal family.

On the plane, I decided to document the shtetl, as a model of the vanished past, on two levels: to present it an exhibit and a book where I would document its nine hundred-year history. For the exhibit, I would not use a single photo taken by a German propaganda photographer or any other photographer with a subjective attitude towards Jewish life in general and East European Jews in particular. I would use photos that show

how people presented themselves. In my book, I would not yield to any political pressure nor historical misrepresentation of East European life.

After nine years of extensive research in public and private archives around the globe, after the collection of thousands of photos and documents, and after a visit to Eishyshok, the idea of the structure of the exhibit was born as I stood on the shtetl's mass grave. We could create a tower where visitors would stand in the center and view the town and life around them, experiencing precisely what I had felt on the mass grave. We would call it "The Tower of Life."

Standing on the grass-covered grave, with yellow buttercups dotting the ground everywhere I looked, I found myself riveted to the spot. I could feel my beloved grandmothers Hayya Sonenson and Alte Katz holding on to me, my aunts, cousins, friends, and neighbors pulling at me. And I could hear the voices of those buried beneath my feet. By this stage of my research, I had read many of their diaries and letters, collected their birth and marriage certificates, and pored over their photographs. They surrounded me now—my family, my parents' friends, and my own little friends—asking me with new urgency to be remembered, not as heaps of skulls and bones, but as the vibrant, dynamic people I'd known. They wanted the world to see them as they had looked at their weddings, on their picnics, in their social clubs, and during the course of their daily lives. During my long vigil at the killing field, Ezekiel's vision of the valley of dry bones had assumed a new meaning to me. "Behold," he heard the Lord say to the bones, "I will cause breath to enter into you, and ye shall live. And I will lay sinews upon you, and will bring up flesh upon you, and cover you with skin, and put breath in you, and ye shall live…"

I offered my idea to prominent people at Yad Vashem, the Museum of the Diaspora in Tel-Aviv, and the interior designers of the United States Holocaust Memorial Museum in Washington, D.C. Martin Smith, who knew me from my interviews for his documentary the *Struggle for Poland*, sent Cindy Miller to me in March 1987. For eight hours, I shared with her my photos. Cindy Miller said, "I walked away completely stunned. What one saw was the entire vibrancy of a small shtetl."

The same day, Miller wrote to Ralph Applebaum, Martin Smith, Michael Berenbaum, and Shaike Weinberg. The response came in November 1989, and Martin Smith came with Cindy Miller to see the photos. After a fascinating discussion, we moved to a new step. Originally, a tower, shaped like a chimney, was to be an exhibit with Auschwitz photos. But due to my photos and ideas, the interior designers moved into a new direction. After long negotiations, my idea was accepted. I gave my photos as a present to the museum. The research of the Tower cost me hundreds of thousands of dollars. To assure historical accuracy, my lawyer Alvin Deutsch stipulated that I would participate in every element regarding the display of my photos. To accommodate my exhibit, the floor between two levels was opened; from the third floor to the fifth floor, the exhibit was narrowed slightly on each level.

When the U.S. Holocaust Memorial Museum opened in April 1993 in Washington, D.C, the Tower became a powerful space because it was the only presentation of life in the museum. The reaction to my exhibit by the millions of visitors to the museum, eighty-four percent of them non-Jews, is very moving. The

Tower has become a model of the universal family of mankind. Many visitors remark, "we never realized that the Jewish people were normal people just like us."

The Tower has become a photographic inspiration. People from around the globe, regardless of their ethnicity and religion, are constantly asking me for photos. Photos from the Tower have become part of the Holocaust Education Center in Fukuyama, Japan.

Prof. Marianne Hirsch wrote in her book about photography entitled *Family Frames*: "My first reaction similar to that of many others, was to marvel at how rich and varied of a life was destroyed. The pictures gain by their diversity and their multiplicity. After looking at them for a while, it became less important to see individual images than to take in a sense of the whole, and of its relation to one's own family album. 'Look, look, look,' I hear people saying all around me, 'we have a picture just like this one in our album.' Or, 'Look, that looks just like grandma!' Interestingly, in the minutes I spend in the [Tower] I find that this identification easily transcends ethnic identity and family history."

In 1998, another aspect of my vision was realized in the form of a book which I had been working on for nineteen years, entitled *There Once Was A World: A 900-Year Chronicle of the Shtetl of Eishyshok*, a National Book Award Finalist. Like the museum's exhibit, the book has helped people to transcend the stereotypes of the Jews of the shtetl, to see them in the fullness of their humanity, not simply as quaint characters in a *Fiddler on the Roof* production or emaciated victims in concentration camp photos.

But as a scholar of East European intellectual history, I know that the portrait of a small town of Eastern European Jewry is still not complete. To really understand that living world in its entirety would involve walking its streets, visiting its houses, and strolling its market squares. This, of course, is an impossibility, since that world was laid waste by the Nazis and their local collaborators. And this is why I decided to build, in the state of Israel, a life-size replica of the shtetl whose history I have documented in my book and whose faces fill the Tower of Life. Comparable in scope and purpose to the recreation of colonial life that has attracted millions of visitors to Williamsburg, Virginia, the shtetl restoration will bring to life a vanished past, and will cast light on the ways in which that bygone world lives on in the culture and institutions of its descendants, now scattered around the globe.

Now my Tower of Life will come to life in the Open-Air Shtetl Museum where the vanished past will be restored.

—Prof. Yaffa Eliach, New York

What's in a Name?

How do you pronounce OhÉigeartaigh? If you're not sure, you're not alone. Bonus points to you if you figured out that it's pronounced o-HEG-are-tea, more commonly recognized as "Hegarty" or "O'Hegarty."

Some twenty-five years ago, I decided to change the spelling of my surname back to the original Gaelic, or as I prefer to call it, Irish. While I didn't have any documented proof of the old spelling in my family, I knew that OhÉigeartaigh was the traditional spelling that it had been used for centuries before English law required the Anglicization of all surnames in Ireland. It wasn't until the Gaelic revival in the 1890s that some families returned to the original spelling of their names. My family retained the English version until I decided to reverse history in 1975.

Growing up in Boston with an immigrant father with an IRA past, I naturally absorbed many tales of British injustices in Ireland. My mother was the daughter of Irish immigrants and had raised money for the IRA. While I wasn't raised to be revolutionary or a rebel, I was keenly aware of the hardships my family had endured in the "old country." My father was very insistent that I develop an appreciation for other cultures, perhaps because he knew what it was to live in an environment where one's culture is barely tolerated.

I took my father's advice to heart and majored in Spanish in college, which made me even hungrier to learn about other cultures and languages. Not surprisingly, one of the languages I chose to master was Irish. Today I teach Irish classes and am very pleased that the demand is so strong.

But it was in 1975 that I decided to take the step of resuming use of the original spelling of my name. As a bit of a compromise, I decided not to use the accent mark over the first e in my name since Americans aren't accustomed to dealing with accents.

At the time of my decision, I was married with two children. My children were too young to weigh in with an opinion, but my wife was less than thrilled at the prospect of adopting the thirteen-letter variation of our name. Respecting my wishes, she eventually relented and agreed to the change. It was my father's opinion, though, that was of greatest concern to me. When my father quietly responded that the "new" spelling was "the way it was supposed to be," my decision was made.

I hired an attorney and went through the usual formalities, placing a notice in the newspaper and filing documentation at the county courthouse. The request was never questioned and my family and I were now legally OhEigeartaigh.

I'm frequently asked whether it's all been worth it. Isn't it a hassle having to constantly spell my name? Isn't it annoying to hear it mispronounced time and time again? Isn't it tedious having to explain that, no, it's not Arabic? No, I don't think so. A surprising number of people of all ethnic persuasions pronounce it correctly the first time, and after a quarter of a century, I've learned to adapt to any minor inconvenience it might cause. When I travel to Ireland, where many others have reverted to the original spelling, I attract no comment as an American bearing the Irish spelling.

I believe that a name is a label that we put on ourselves, and I consider my decision to be like that of many African Americans who use names that reflect their cultural heritage. But I don't see it as a statement and I find it curious that it is so frequently a subject of discussion. Given my awareness of the injustices that first forced my family to shift to the Anglicized Hegarty spelling, though, I suppose it is somewhat appropriate that OhEigeartaigh translates to "unjust"—a quiet protest hidden in my name.

—*Richard OhEigeartaigh, Massachusetts*

Photo copyright Johnson's Photography, courtesy of Makoché Recording Company. Used with permission.

A Message in Music

Being an Indian singer, people expect certain things, but I don't want to be limited in what I can sing about. My Indian heritage is part of who I am, so some of it comes out in my music. Like all of us, I'm influenced by my surroundings—I'm a product of my environment.

I was born and raised on an Ojibwe Indian reservation in Northern Minnesota, but I also lived on both coasts and in Japan while serving in the Marines, so I sing about a variety of human conditions I've seen and experienced: Love is hard to find and should be cherished; we need to care for children wherever they are in the world; alcoholism and abuse are human problems everywhere; people everywhere are being mined of their spirits and need healing; no one should judge another person by the color of his or her skin.

My music is a gift I can use as a weapon. I just want to tell the truth about the world as I see it. I see a lot of injustice all around, as do we all. I write and sing about it. I guess it's like the old blues legends say, "You can't sing the blues in an air-conditioned room." If I lived in a world where everything was peachy, I wouldn't sing—and that's the truth.

Maybe I get some of it from my mother, Anne Dunn. She has always been a storyteller. She's creative and encouraged me to create. She encouraged me to love adventure. And if you think like her, everything is an adventure—even getting a flat tire. She taught me that everything happens for a reason. She taught me that faith is a powerful thing. A real thing. And she always told me, "Don't let anyone treat you like a squaw."

Several songs on my last release *The Heron Smiled* reflect my mother's influence and our Anishinaabe heritage. "Spirit Horses," based on my mother's story about a boy who learns a dream song and uses it to call spirit horses, tells of the tribe's hope for a child of this generation to learn its song.

And "500 Years," a much-needed song about 500 years of genocide, was inspired by my mother. She and I wrote the lyrics with Carson Gardner. It speaks of many people, places and injustices. Some are in the history books like Columbus, Encomiendo, and Jamestown. But it also speaks of lesser-known heroics. It talks of Jean Brave Heart, who works to protect the wolf in Minnesota even with brain cancer. And of Jim "Iron Legs" Weaver, who walked across the country when he was in his seventies to bring attention to the poisoning of the Mississippi River. He walked all the way to the White House and waited out front. It also talks of Ingrid Washinawatok, who was murdered by the Colombian Revolutionary Armed Forces (FARC) while in Colombia to assist the U'wa Indians in developing a traditional school that would protect their culture. She was an architect of peace and a woman of Earth.

A person could learn a lot by researching every place, person, and event in this eight-minute song. Maybe the words will inspire people to pay more attention to the past. Awareness is important in fighting prejudice.

At the end of the song, I sing about the red oak, the one tree that holds its leaves all winter. Like the red oak leaves, we will always be here because the strength of the people and our ancestors is hidden in our DNA.

And if you think about it, that applies to all of us. If you go back far enough, all people come from tribes. People chanted, played hand drums, prayed in lodges, and lived with the Earth. Everyone who's reading these words comes from a tribe and we all share the same DNA that our ancestors carried within them. Their memories are still in us. With my music, I hope to create a memory for my own descendants.

—*Annie Humphrey, Minnesota*

Three-Generation Boots

Thirty by eighty feet is a lot of space to explore, but I was intrigued by the possibilities and I already knew what to paint.

My family always told tales of our past, and when we would go on vacation, we'd inevitably end up at some ancestor's old home or a place where a great-great-grandfather came from. After I moved to New York to pursue a graduate degree at the School of Visual Arts, I began thinking about where I came from and where my roots were. I realized that I didn't have a specific landscape that I could identify with as my home. My family moved around a lot when I was growing up, and I found myself contemplating landscape as an identity. It dawned on me that my ancestors could be my roots, that I could say, "this is who I am."

Not surprisingly, my art began to reflect my interest in roots. The summer after my first year of graduate school, I decided I wanted to see all the vital, genealogical information written on the wall of my studio. I was interested in the shape that the information would take—both the known information and the information that was not there—and somehow that shape would become something of a self-portrait.

Fortunately, much of my family history had already been researched, so I was able to acquaint myself with many generations of ancestors within a matter of months. Starting with myself, I worked backward and copied the names of thousands of ancestors onto the walls, ceiling, and floor of my studio.

Living with all these names, I realized I really liked this project and wanted to add some images. Using old photos and my own impressions of my ancestors' places of origin, I began painting their stories, focusing on both my matriarchal and patriarchal lines.

Before long, I was invited to recreate this project to a gallery in Soho, and then I received a grant to go to Norway for two months. Intending to do a project on these ancestors, I did watercolors of where they lived and researched libraries and photo archives for more clues about these people.

When I returned, I was invited by the Queens Museum of Art in Flushing, New York, to inaugurate the use of an eighty-foot wall, the wedge created by two ramps connecting the museum's first and second floors, as a canvas. It was a non-conventional space, to be sure, but I was attracted to the triangular shape because I thought it would lend itself to my work in terms of telling an ancestral story.

Using my sketches. I painted "Family in Norway," essentially

141

Photos copyright Jean Vong. Used with permission.

a very large, upside-down pedigree chart. Starting at the narrowest point of the giant wedge, I painted Ragna Johnson, my great-grandmother, as she was the most recent immigrant. Opting to break away from the confines of a normal pedigree chart, I continued Ragna's maternal line along the top and her paternal line along the bottom. According to the geography of Norway, my maternal ancestors lived in the northernmost part of the country, so I wanted them to be at the highest point.

All through the wall painting, I intermingled people and places, since the landscape was such an integral part of their existence. And I incorporated family stories, such as the three-generation boots. My great-great-great-grandfather, Olaus Johnson, was a shoemaker whose boots were said to be so sturdy that they would last for three generations. Starting knee high, they could simply be cut down over the years as the leather wore out. So three boots of varying heights appear in the mural, each one supporting a house, ship, or religious tract. These unexpected juxtapositions symbolize an episode when the family was forced to move, and chose to take their house, broken down board by board, under sail to a new city where it still stands today.

As I started on this project, the fragile black and white images, text, and stories brittle with age began to transform in my mind. Color like breath inflated the images and gave them new life. All the stories and ancestors took new strength and form. Although still two dimensional, I felt that the lively ancestors were pleased with their new existence in the show.

—*Valerie Atkisson, New York*

142

A Place to
Call Home

As a child, I lived the nomadic life of an "Army brat." I've never understood what this term is meant to imply, but it refers to those of us who spent much of our youth moving from one Army base to another. Over the course of our assignments, I attended six elementary schools and three high schools. As the perpetual new student, I was often asked, "Where do you come from?" With a little difficulty I would try to explain that I came from all over the place. I was born in New York and moved six months later to another state, and then kept moving about every other year. This usually just brought confused looks from the other students, many of whom had lived in the same town since birth. Years later, I found myself asking the same question: "Where do I come

143

from?" I needed a place to call home and a better answer than simply, "all over the place."

It was about this time that the first genealogy software programs began appearing. With this tool to organize my information and a deep yearning to find my roots, I was off in earnest to find my ancestors. After several years and a collection of a few thousand names in my computer, I had traced my Scottish lineage to a small town in southern Ayrshire called Maybole. Having spent many hours documenting my ancestral connections to the town, I wanted to learn more about its history and exchange information with others of Maybole descent. I spent days surfing the Internet. Maybole, however, is a small community with a population of less than five thousand, in the somewhat remote lowlands of Scotland. There was not much to be found, and living in Florida, I would have to cross the Atlantic Ocean if I wanted to visit in person.

Then it occurred to me that instead of scouring the world for bits of Maybole history and new cousins, I could let them come to me! I had just created a website with some of my family history data, so why not set up another site where those with Maybole ancestry could exchange information? Certainly our ancestors deserved to be put on the Internet map!

I assumed that all the domain names for the town had been taken by cyberspace speculators, but because of the town's relatively small size, a good selection was still available. I registered maybole.org and launched a small site for family historians.

Not long after this I was in e-mail contact with the chairman of the Maybole Community Council, David Kiltie. After an exchange of a few messages, David asked me if I was "prepared

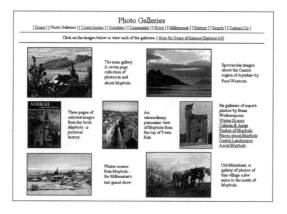

to see the site expanded." There was in fact an amazing wealth of local history information available. Over the centuries, many writers had documented Maybole's long and fascinating story. But the books, documents, photographs, family histories, and other mementos of the past were scattered among assorted libraries, in the hands of local organizations and citizens, or sprinkled around the globe to all those places to which Maybole's citizenry had emigrated. And none of it was on the Internet. That was two years ago.

Today, with over 750 pages and several thousand images, www.maybole.org is one of the largest community-based websites in Scotland. It documents the town's past as well as the lives and spirit of its citizens today. The site is the result of the cooperative effort of the residents of Maybole, Maybole's extended Internet community, and in no small measure, David Kiltie.

And there is no end in sight. Each month, more local citizens and organizations become involved and discoveries of historical treasures continue to be made. A local plumber recently came forward with a register of the local Maybole militia from the late 1800s, providing great details about its members including

145

their signatures. A neighborhood of Maybole expatriates in Hamilton, Canada, produced a 1920s panoramic photo of a group living in an area there known as Little Maybole. A local minister found a large, black metal box with documents going back several centuries in the church attic. And the list goes on. A search of antiquarian booksellers on the Internet led to the purchase of local Maybole history books from New Zealand, Australia, Canada, and other countries to which Maybole citizens carried or sent them. Many of these have yet to be scanned and placed on the site, but will provide new material for years to come. The website is now a source of civic pride and truly a community effort, composed of contributions from hundreds of individuals.

My original objectives in starting the website—to learn more about this place my ancestors called home and make connections with other researchers—were long ago met and surpassed. Maybole is definitely on the Internet map—just check any search engine! But I am still thrilled when we receive comments such as these:

> *I have just recently started searching into my family history and have found your site and the Maybole pages. I was so excited as my grandparents are from Maybole and they came to the States in 1907. I see the pictures and read the history and it is like I am walking in the footsteps of my grandmother. I am located in a small town in Wyoming so the Internet is the only source of information.*

> *It will be my pleasure to travel to the beautiful place my ancestors called home hopefully one day soon. Through your site I can actually visualize their homeland. Frankly, it seems difficult to imagine why they would leave such a pretty place.*

I live in Christchurch, New Zealand, and am so excited tonight to discover the wonderful Maybole site. My forebears left Maybole for New Zealand in 1876.... It is brilliant being able to see so many clear photos of the town and to get a feel from the other side of the world for my roots.... You've made one Maybole descendant very happy.

I have been very honored to be part of the Maybole community. In April 2001, on my first visit to my ancestral hometown, I was named citizen of the year for my role in the Maybole website, an award I will cherish as long as I live. I believe that our Maybole ancestors would feel pride in our tribute to the spirit of their homeland and would be honored to see that the legacy they have given us is cherished and made available for the rest of the world. A similar tribute to the town and its heritage was made over a hundred years ago in a book written by one of the most prolific of those chronicling the life and history of the town, the Rev. Roderick Lawson. The sentiments so well expressed in the preface to his book are as appropriate today as they were then, in 1885.

He wrote: "Maybole may appear commonplace to others, but to those whose life's history has been connected with it, the old town must ever be surrounded by a halo.... There have been tragedies and comedies here as elsewhere, and the history of a town is but as the history of the world at large. I trust that natives of Maybole [and their descendants], who are scattered abroad, may be pleased to have this memento of the place of their birth.... Everybody should take an interest in the place where his lot is cast; and one of my aims will be served if it helps...to promote the well-being of the "little city of our dwelling which we belong to on this side of the grave." And my highest aim will be attained, if it helps in any wise to teach the sacredness of home, as the spot where our life-tragedy has been appointed us, and which must therefore ever have an interest to us over all other places."

I have lived in my own community of about the same size as Maybole's for almost twenty years. It's a great place to live and I'm developing a website for it as well, but I know more of the history of the land of my ancestors than I do of my own place of residence. And now if someone asks me where I come from, I have an answer.

—*Rich Pettit, Florida*

Ending the Witch Hunt

My interest in family history began in the early 1990s when I came across some copies of letters from my husband's grandmother. These letters prompted us to begin researching Pete's family. After learning about his Revolutionary War ancestors and those who had been missionaries in India, I wistfully commented that I wished I had some interesting ancestors. Pete encouraged me to begin researching my family in earnest.

In 1994, I learned that my eighth great-grandmother, Susanna North Martin, had been executed as a witch in 1692 in Salem, Massachusetts. Accused of "sundry acts of witchcraft" ranging from casting a hex on neighbors' cows to riding a broomstick through a rainstorm, Susanna had insistently proclaimed her innocence, but her protests failed to save her from the gallows. Apparently, my request for interesting ancestors had been heard.

I was born and raised in New England and had grown up on tales of the Salem witches. In my naiveté, I thought of these unfortunate folks as old crones who dabbled in the black arts with brooms and cats, but now I began to read anything I could find related to the Salem witchcraft hysteria in an effort to truly know Susanna and the times in which she lived and died.

As I read, a very different picture emerged. Born in 1621 in England, she came to America with her father, stepmother, and at least one sister. I began to imagine Susanna as a girl sailing to New England with her family. Her bold personality in later years suggests that even as a youngster, she was probably very brave and thought of this journey as a great adventure. She married George Martin, a blacksmith, in 1646 and had eight children. I thought of her as a wife and mother, making a home and raising her children in the face of many challenges.

Descriptions of Susanna say that she was short, slightly plump, and active. Like several others of the accused, she was an outspoken widow who owned a great deal of land. Charges of witchcraft were first lodged against her more than twenty years earlier in 1669, but they were dropped and her husband, who was still alive at the time, had successfully sued for slander.

Never a quiet conformist to begin with, this previous experience left Susanna contemptuous of authority and defiant in the face of the false accusations that surfaced in 1692. Although she clearly understood the seriousness of her situation, she ridiculed much of the "evidence" used against her and laughed out loud when "afflicted girls" began having fits in the courtroom during her trial. When asked why she had laughed, she replied, "Well, I may at such folly."

During her examination, Susanna was asked if she had lied. She replied, "I dare not tell a lie if it would save my life." The irony is, had she lied, confessed to being a witch and repented, her life most probably would have been spared.

Not everyone was taken in by the hysteria of the times. In his *History of Amesbury*, Joseph Merrill says, "The idea of snatching this hardworking, honest woman from her home to be tried for her life by those who never knew her, and witnesses who were prejudiced against her... is almost too much for belief... . Allowed no counsel, she was her own lawyer, and her answers are remarkable for independence and clearness. She showed herself to be a woman of more than ordinary talent and resolution."

But old grudges and Susanna's plain speaking—a trait apparent in some tart-tongued women in my family today—were enough to convict her. As I soaked up all these details about her life and times, I developed a deep affection for her and often wondered if I would have had her strength of character in the circumstances she endured. Would I have had the courage to speak my mind?

In early 1999, I was surprised to discover that Susanna and four others—Bridget Bishop, Margaret Scott, Alice Parker, and Wilmot Redd—had never been exonerated of the crime of witchcraft. In 1711, a general amnesty had been issued and absolved all but six of the accused witches. More than two hundred years later, Chapter 145 of the Resolves of 1957 cleared the name of Ann Pudeator who had been hanged, but made no mention of the remaining five.

Seeking to learn more about this situation, I came in contact with Paula Gauthier Keene, who was working to have these women legally exonerated. Thus I found myself part of an online campaign to get as many people as possible to contact state legislators and urge the passage of House Bill 2752 to clear the names of Salem's forgotten five. Radio and newspaper interviews also helped bring attention to these women. Just a few short years earlier, I never would have imagined myself involved in an effort to rectify a three-hundred-year-old injustice, but now, nothing seemed more natural or necessary.

I strongly believed that Susanna, who had gone to her death protesting her innocence, would not rest in peace until her name was cleared. Many people are baffled by my efforts and say, "What difference does it make? She'll never know." But if you believe in an afterlife as I do, you have to believe that she would know and care.

Our campaign finally resulted in Susanna's long overdue vindication. On 31 October 2001, Massachusetts Acting Governor Jane Swift signed House Bill 2752 which became Chapter 122 of the Acts of 2001. After 309 years, Susanna, Bridget, Margaret, Alice, and Wilmot have finally been exonerated! When I heard the news, I cried tears of joy. These Christian souls can now rest in peace.

The most crucial work is done, but the efforts to honor Susanna and the others who suffered during the witchcraft hysteria will continue. Paula is organizing a memorial service in Salem and I will be working with her to have a memorial established on Gallows Hill. We can't undo history, but we can at least rewrite this little piece of it.

—*Bonnie Johnson, Maryland*

SAMUEL POSTLETHWAITE
PVT   CO D 21 MISS INF
CONFEDERATE STATES ARMY
APR 6 1833   AUG 20 1876

A Confederate in New England

A bout ten years ago, on a frozen Sunday afternoon, I began to contemplate where I might vacation if summer were kind enough to someday return. My intention was to tour several Civil War battlefields. Limited to two weeks, my wife and I decided to visit the library to research likely sites and plan the most efficient travel route. This casual visit to the library was the inadvertent first step in unraveling a complex and compelling story.

One book, a detailed, state-by-state guide to the Civil War, suited my needs perfectly. I began by glancing through the Rhode Island section of the book and was struck by a reference that seemed completely out of place: "Greenwood Cemetery has the grave of a Confederate soldier, Samuel Postlethwaite. At present the grave site has an unmarked stone to the right of the William Rogers Greene stone."

A Confederate? Was he a Rhode Islander? Why was he buried here? Out of simple curiosity, my wife and I decided to drive the twenty minutes to the cemetery and see the humble grave for ourselves. The cemetery was much larger than expected, and finding the stone of William Rogers Greene seemed hopeless in the gathering darkness. Failing to locate it that day, I returned to the cemetery until I found the grave in question, but Samuel Postlethwaite's space to the right was occupied only by grass.

So began my quest to solve the mystery of a Confederate soldier buried in Rhode Island. I didn't know then that I was embarking on a research project that would consume several years and require at least a dozen trips to the South. As I explored countless sources throughout the United States, a story would slowly emerge. I would walk the battlefields on which this soldier had fought and the fields he had plowed. Gradually, "Sam," as I began to call him, would come to life for me, a fascinating figure who by accident of fate became part of one of Rhode Island's most famous families.

The research was difficult, but fortunately, I had the foresight to marry a librarian. With my wife's help, I compiled a list of relevant media outlets and sent brief blurbs about the mystery. Happily, Sam's story began to attract attention and letters started pouring in, so much so that we started calling it "Sam mail." When his obituary, detailing his experience at the Seven Days' Battle at Malvern Hill arrived one day, I felt an instant bond with this poor fellow who had been so entirely forgotten.

154

Soon I began traveling to the battle-fields where Sam had served. Walking down these fields was eerie, especially seeing the trenches, woods, and hills that were exactly as they had been described in all my readings. Our bond grew stronger. Everywhere I went, I found myself thinking, "Gee Sam, what were you thinking of when you were here?"

As time went on, people would ask me how "the Sam thing" was going. One night, a friend told me, "You're going to have to write a book about this." I shrugged the suggestion off, as my only intention was to put a marker on Sam's grave, but over time, I began to reconsider. My story had become so inter-twined with Sam's that it appealed to me to share both of our experiences.

So I wrote *Lost Soul: The Confederate Soldier in New England* and explained how it was that Sam came to rest in Rhode Island. His connection to the North was through his sister, Mollie, who married a Rhode Islander, William Greene. In fact, my favorite part of the book is when Mollie and William meet.

Mollie was staying at a rooming house in Vicksburg, Mississippi, not long after the war when she heard that a Yankee was staying there as well. Still resentful of the ruin of Sam's health and the imprisonment of another brother, Mollie quietly protested by refusing to come to dinner while the Yankee was in the house. But one day, she spied him out the window playing with her aunt's children and decided that per-haps he wasn't such a bad fellow after all. When she went to dinner that evening, it was a classic case of love at first sight, and Mollie soon found herself engaged to a Northerner. It was this relationship between William and Mollie that ultimately brought Sam to Rhode Island, resulting in his burial so far from his Southern home.

It is also this part of the story that symbolizes the whole book. William and Mollie's relationship symbolize how ignorance may be overcome. They chose forgiveness and understanding over bitterness and hatred. In my mind, they were the real heroes.

By the mid-1990s, after writing countless letters to various veteran groups, the Department of Veterans Affairs offered to issue a bronze grave marker for Sam. Finally, on Veteran's Day in 1994, a ceremony was held giving Sam the recognition he deserved, but even I was surprised by the number of people who attended.

Retired Senator Claiborne Pell of Rhode Island could not attend, but sent a letter to be read at the service: "A Civil War soldier dies after reversals of fortune and illness in a place far distant from his home; more than a century later his service and the location of his grave stimulate research by an unrelated man; and by this extraordinary connection between two men, the vitality of history is made manifest."

As a result of Sam, I've gained compassion for others, a better understanding of people who are different from me, and a deep sense of how important a legacy is and how you want people to remember you. I now write and lecture on this no longer lost soul and the importance of historic preservation in general. In the hunt for Sam's life, I have found new purpose in my own.

—*Les Rolston, Rhode Island*

Quilting Quandary

Since childhood, I have been obsessed with both needlework and genealogy, so I suppose it was inevitable that I'd eventually combine the two.

Last year, I was very excited to locate a cousin of my late husband's grandfather via the Internet. This wonderful gentleman kindly shared old photos of folks for whom our family had not even known names. Organizing this new-found collection of ancestral treasures inspired me to begin a quilt, but I immediately found myself in a bit of quandary.

Any family historian knows that genealogical research is never truly finished, since ongoing research is sure to add more family members, so how was I to construct a quilt that could accommodate future discoveries? I solved the problem by focusing specifically on those family members for whom I have a photo and giving each one his own mini-quilt, a ten by fourteen-inch block with finished edges. Then I decided to join these blocks together using velcro, affording me the opportunity for unlimited future additions.

Photos copyright Pat Flynn Kyser. Used with permission.

I also applied the color-coding method I use for all my research to the quilt-in-progress. All folders and notebooks in my maternal Tracy line are red, so all the mini-quilts for Tracy ancestors have red bindings. My paternal Flynn line has yellow edges, while my husband's maternal Sawyer line has blue and his paternal Kyser line has green. This color-coding scheme makes it easy to see where each ancestor fits into the greater family. Pockets on the back of each ancestor block hold a laminated card with a short biography of that person.

I chose to do the blocks in the crazy quilt style, a Victorian-era form of needlework in which bits of randomly shaped fabrics are sewn together. Each seam is then covered with elaborate embroidery work, strips of lace, or ribbon. Finally, the odd-shaped pieces become palettes for embroidery, beadwork, or painting.

Some of the pieces within each block are composed of fabric containing old photos of my ancestors. In some cases, there is only one photograph. In others, I am fortunate enough to have both childhood and adult photos. A picture of my grandfather's birth cottage in County Kerry, Ireland, adorns his block, while in another, I used a photo of a quilt made by my husband's great-great-grandmother. We hang it behind our Christmas tree each year, so it seemed appropriate to add to her block.

I took my collection of pictures to the local copy shop to help with the photo-to-fabric transfer. The equipment allowed me to have each image made to an ideal size for its block.

Because I know so little about some of the ancestors, I did not attempt to make the needlework on each block biographical. Instead, I called upon my years of experience and embellished to my heart's content. Occasionally, I embroidered wild flowers from the ancestor's home state or added a flag or charm that represented his military service or some other aspect of life. I added an old advertising "cigarette silk" with a damsel representing Ireland, for instance, to my Grandfather Flynn's block.

To serve as the anchor for my ancestral quilt, I made a banner emblazoned with my belief that "They live so long as we remember." A dowel inserted into a sleeve on the back of the banner supports the entire quilt, and the mini-quilts hang in rows beneath it.

The quilt now graces the entry hall to my home where it evokes comments and questions each time a visitor arrives—and gives me leeway to share the lives of my ancestors with my guests. At present, it has thirteen blocks, but numbers fourteen and fifteen are in process as I write these words. Now that I've solved the challenge of designing a quilt that can grow along with my expanding family tree, I can honestly say that I hope this is one quilt that will never be finished.

—*Pat Flynn Kyser, Alabama*

911:
Roots and Wings

The following eulogy was given by Richard Deuel on January 12, 2002 for his twenty-eight-year-old sister, Cindy Deuel, who was killed in the World Trade Center on September 11, 2001. Cindy was an avid genealogist who was passionately seeking her roots up to the day of the disaster, and Richard was her family history partner. She had even dreamed of starting a genealogy business to help people with their own family research. Richard is commissioning a specially crafted headstone with Cindy's family tree on one side (much of it information she learned through her own efforts) and the Twin Towers on the other. He also chose a particularly meaningful place for Cindy's burial. The site, pictured above with Cindy and Richard, is the rediscovered gravesite of their ancestor and the place Cindy was buried some eighteen months after the photo was taken.

I'd like to share with everyone why we chose Cedar Lawn Cemetery for Cindy. It wasn't long ago that Cindy and I stood over this very spot, as we posed for a picture to document the final resting place of our great-great-grandfather, Henry Deuel. Cindy found this spot even though there is no headstone to mark his grave. Many have asked how she was able to find Henry, who was interred here in 1874.

As with everything Cindy did in life, she was fired with an unlimited determination, guided by a passion for a good mystery, and inspired by a love of things historical. Most importantly, she was touched by the lives of the families of those who walked before—those forgotten men, women, and children who paved the path for us. Every time Cindy and I scanned a pre-1900 census record, we knew the thousands of names slowly scrolling by were no longer with us. A respectful sadness makes you want to know about these people, especially your ancestors.

And the more you learn, the more you want to know. Our great-grandfather, John J. Deuel, was just one of these people. He ran a poolroom and tobacco shop on Main Avenue in Passaic, New Jersey in the early 1880s. Cindy was scanning the Passaic newspaper for advertisements he had placed. That was when she found an obituary for John's infant son, George. The paper mentioned George was interred at Cedar Lawn. With one call to Cedar Lawn, Cindy then learned who else was buried with John's son in the same plot. She had found our great-great-grandfather, Henry.

How Cindy loved Henry! We could talk about him for hours on end. Where was Henry from? Who was Henry's father? We would spend hours at the library looking for him in census records. I used to buy O'Henry candy bars in the hope it would bring us luck in finding out about him. I got the biggest kick when I found out that Cindy followed my lead and also started snacking on O'Henrys.

Henry is still a mystery to me, but no longer to Cindy. Along with Henry's grandchild, George, who is buried here, there are twin boys, Henry and John. All three died as infants—like Cindy, long before their time. Cindy is now their guardian angel.

We chose Cedar Lawn because the people Cindy brought back to "life" are buried here, some of whom made it possible for Cindy to come into our lives. Some others here at Cedar Lawn are our great-grandmother, Maggie Deuel, and our grandfather's sister, Annie Deuel, someone my father and his siblings didn't even know about until I discovered her two months ago. She named one of her sons, of course, Henry John. Also there is our great-great uncle, Arthur Costantini, who came over from Italy. Also next door at Cavalry Cemetery is—yes, I will say it—Grandpa's first wife, Anna Earle, and his first son, John.

As we stand here above the Deuel plot, I think of Grandpa's three siblings who are buried here. What if Grandpa was the one who had died as an infant instead of these brothers? Then most of us would evaporate from this scene. I think of our great-grandmother, Maggie. Both she and her mother had fifteen children. As an old woman, in some twisted, cosmic joke, Maggie died a horrible death in a kitchen fire. And then there's Grandpa's first son, John, who died at age twenty-two when he fell out of a window.

Cindy understood this rhythm of life, the uncertainty that goes along with it, and was not afraid of anything. I admired that quality about her more than any other. Cindy's favorite movie was *Contact* with Jodie Foster. In it, the character Jodie Foster plays loses her father as a young girl. She then spends her life searching boundless space for any sounds of life. When she does make contact and travels to the source, it is in the form of her father, telling her that we all must take baby steps toward understanding, and that one day it will all make sense. Her father always assured her there was more life out there, because if there weren't, it would be a great waste of space.

One of the last things Cindy asked was if we thought she would ever get to travel in space. I believe that is where she is now, soaring on the wings of comets, exploring strange new worlds and life forms, and truly going where no woman has ever gone before.

—Richard Deuel, New York

Playing for Keeps

On a brisk, early autumn evening in 1999, my husband and I were seated on a small hillside outside Clay, West Virginia, eagerly awaiting the start of a play called *Solomon's Secret*. This wasn't just another play, it was a "home-grown" drama about part of my own family history. Apparently not only relatives were interested because the hill was full of people waiting for the story to unfold.

This production wasn't always a public one. In fact, it really didn't start as a full-fledged play at all. Instead, in 1991, members of the Bib Osborne family were looking for a way to teach their children about their Cherokee heritage and they decided to do it by way of a short play at their family reunion. At first, the play was very simple and lasted only ten to fifteen minutes. But that was long enough to give an overview of Solomon and Seaberry Osborne's trek from western North Carolina in the late 1830s to their final destination in Clay County, West Virginia, a decade later.

The children weren't totally unaware of their heritage. In the family's possession is a photograph of Solomon wearing both white and Indian clothing. They'd heard some of the stories, and some of the elders could count in the Cherokee language. Sometimes it was said that a certain method of doing things was the "Cherokee way."

Some members of the family, Vickie Osborne Brown, Ann Osborne, Janeen Osborne, and others, had been researching the Osborne genealogy. It wasn't always easy to find documentation since Solomon and Seaberry were considered federal fugitives because they moved to avoid the forced removal of the Cherokees from the Smoky Mountains to Indian Territory west of the Mississippi. Through the years, members of the family were discrete about their heritage and tried to appear part of the mainstream white culture. However, the family always knew who they were, even if the details weren't all there.

Through their research, the Osbornes found more details about the migration of Solomon and Seaberry. Beginning near the Oconaluftee River in western North Carolina, they traced a trail that led first to Prather Creek in Ashe County, North Carolina. There they found church records that listed Seaberry Osborne as a member. Next, they found a cabin in Tazewell, Virginia, that Solomon Osborne had built for his growing family. The cabin still exists and is on the Virginia registry of historical places. From there, Solomon and Seaberry moved with a group of relatives to Wyoming County in what is now West Virginia. Not long afterward, they relocated in Clay County, West Virginia, where at last the migration stopped.

Photos courtesy of Victoria Osborne Brown and Shannon Bibb Brown. Used with permission.

After uncovering this long and tortured journey, and with the excitement of finding their ancestor's cabin, several members of the Osborne family felt that they needed a better way to share what they'd learned. They'd already begun to be more open about their Native American heritage, but that wasn't enough to keep all that had been discovered from possibly being lost again.

In the end, several family members decided to present a short drama at the family reunion. Not only could a larger audience be reached, but it would be an especially good way to teach the children. From its abbreviated beginnings, more scenes were added along with some original music and lyrics.

In a small town not much stays secret. Word got out about this innovative family's reunion drama and they were encouraged to present it to the public. Since that first little play in 1991, the Osborne family has performed at various locations throughout West Virginia including schools, powwows, and the Tammarack Visitor's Center. From 1995 until the present, *Solomon's Secret* has also been produced in conjunction with Clay County's Golden Delicious Apple Festival.

Nearly all of the sixty or so people it takes to put on this now nearly two-hour play are family members. The actors are anywhere from grade school kids to grandparents and range from fourth to eighth generation descendants. All are volunteers and any money made from donations goes to produce the play.

These folks don't pretend to be professional thespians; they just want to share their pride in their family history.

Watching part of my family story unfold before me that crisp fall evening was a sight I'll never forget. Not only did I feel pride in my ancestry, but I was also happy to know that this generation was doing something to teach the next about who they are and where they came from. Our history isn't just in dry charts and family trees. It's out there being shared for the generations to come.

—*Susan Cruikshank Hanna, New York*

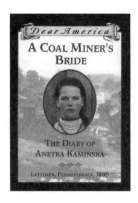

Our Mother Lode

As a writer, I have a tendency to look for stories everywhere—in books and movies, in newspapers and on the news, and in conversations with people. I'm especially drawn to stories about my ancestors and the ancestors of others from the anthracite coal region of Pennsylvania.

For the most part, I'm a product of Pennsylvania's anthracite region, a tiny area that measures little more than 1,400 square miles. Here, hard coal—anthracite—was once king. Here, the anthracite industry gave rise to powerful coal bosses, stupendous technological achievements, and bloody labor struggles as it helped transform the United States into the most powerful industrial nation in the world.

The anthracite industry required cheap, expendable labor. Here, immigrants from twenty-six countries transplanted themselves and their families and their old-world ways. Here, immigrant men and young boys toiled long hours in darkness for meager wages. Here, widows and orphans were made when explosions and cave-ins occurred, signaled by the sharp blast of the breaker whistle. The anthracite coal was hard. The lives of the anthracite people were harder.

Yet, here, a story emerges that is uniquely American, full of hardship and sacrifice, but also of triumph and the fulfillment of hopes and dreams. Here, my imagination runs as deep and as rich as the mother lode.

To unearth stories, I mine the mother lode: I dig a lot in my memory and in the memories of other people. Mostly, I do this by collecting oral histories from ordinary people who think their lives had little to do with history. Though I also rely a great deal on historical research, for me, a story begins with the feeling I get about a fact, a feeling that inspires me to search for more information. It is through these feelings that I discover what I'm trying to say and I uncover the extraordinary lives of ordinary people. I owe my mother lode to the strong women in my family and the strong women who formed the backbone of the anthracite region.

In my family, it is the women who are the keepers of stories. My grandmother, Ada Mackinder Reese, was the last of twelve children. She was born with a caul, a membrane that covers the faces of some babies at birth. Many people believed that a baby born with a caul would have the power of divination and would become notorious in some way.

Except for my grandmother's belief in the power of prayer, she didn't have the power of divination. And if my grandmother was notorious for anything, it was her habit of telling the same stories over and over again. An impatient child, I thought

169

there was something wrong with her memory. I heard about her father, a huckster who gave away leftover produce to widows, and how her mother's house was visited by hoboes, who knew they could get a free meal if they knocked at the back door. I heard how Ada and her husband were secretly married for nine months before their families found out. I heard about the Great Depression. Mostly, I heard about her "ladies," the elderly women she took in as boarders as a way of making ends meet after her husband suffered a severe stroke and died.

As an adult, I know there was nothing wrong with my grandmother's memory. She was passing on my family history to me, a history that would not be mine until I knew it by heart.

Though I often step into other cultures and use research to create the details in my work, I reach down inside myself to pull out themes that are very real. In *Dancing with Dziadziu* (Harcourt 1997), I wrote about Gabriella, who loves to hear her grandmother's stories again and again—stories about her emigration to America, her shanty in the coal patch, her chickens with their feet painted blue, and the long-ago Saturday nights when she and her husband were courting. "Babci has told me the story a hundred times, but each time I pretend it's new," says Gabriella. In fiction, authors get to rewrite—fix—past events, and Gabriella is a much more patient child than I.

My mother is another strong woman; she was widowed at the age of twenty-three and left with two young children—my brother, twenty-two months old, and me, two months old. When I started to develop the character of Anetka Kaminska for *A Coal Miner's Bride* (Scholastic 2000), I thought a lot about my spirited redheaded mother and her faith, courage, and resolve. Again, the details of *A Coal Miner's Bride* are products of

170

research and imagination, but I found much of my main character when I mined my mother lode for strong women.

In this novel, thirteen-year-old Anetka Kaminska emigrates from Poland to Lattimer, Pennsylvania, in 1896 as a promised bride to a widowed coal miner. Anetka endures a loveless marriage and other hardships, but she survives because she has *hart ducha*, a spirited heart, just like her mother and grandmother. When Anetka finally confronts her husband, she says, "I suddenly remembered I was Anetka Kaminska, Mamusia's fiery redhead and Babcia's granddaughter who has hart ducha." This is the way it is with our ancestral mother lode. Here we find innate energy, healthy boundaries, and ageless knowing. Here we remember who we are, where we come from, and what we are about.

The anthracite region is filled with stories of strong immigrant girls and women. In my nonfiction photo-essays *Growing Up In Coal Country* and *Kids on Strike!* (Houghton 1996, 1999), I tell the stories of women and children who banded together and fought for better working and living conditions. These stories are important because they show the way our ancestors lived, loved, hoped, believed, and persevered.

I have written a dozen or more books. From my research, I know that strong girls and women are found across all cultures. Each time I mine the mother lode, each time I tell a story, I am honoring the spirit of our mothers and grandmothers.

—*Susan Campbell Bartoletti, Pennsylvania*

171

Smithsteinian

I guess you could say I'm a keeper of the faith—the Jewish faith, that is. I'm not especially observant in the sense of regularly going to synagogue and celebrating the Sabbath, but no one who's ever heard of me would question the pride I feel in my religion and heritage. In fact, some people think I'm slightly obsessed, and I suppose the documentary about me entitled *Obsessed with Jews* doesn't exactly discourage people from adopting this perspective.

Still, what's so strange about collecting memorabilia? I collect items pertaining to Jewish people—mostly famous, but some less so—in entertainment, politics, and sports. Yes, I said sports. Did you know it was a Jew, Ossie Schectman, who scored the first points in the first game in NBA history? My photo of Ossie and a Wheaties box featuring Olympian Kerri Strug (who could ever forget her sticking that landing?) are just as representative of the history of the Jewish people as my autographs of Woody Allen and Yitzhak Rabin.

It started innocently enough in March 1990 with the somewhat predictable purchase of a 1961 Sandy Koufax card. Since then, I have amassed what may well be the largest such collection in the world. At last count, I had more than 12,000 trading cards, autographs, photos, pins, and matchbook covers catalogued in my neatly organized binders and throughout my house. So far, my wife and two daughters have thankfully not balked at competing for space with all the Jewish memorabilia stored in our house.

I have spent thousands of dollars and estimate that I devote an average of ten hours per week to the collection, but even as a professional accountant, I can't begin to calculate the value of something like this. I get great joy from showing my collection at trade shows and Jewish Community Centers, and I believe it's important to increase Jewish pride through role models, to educate everyone about Jewish accomplishments, and to reduce anti-Semitism. Particularly when you think of the anti-Semitism that has been around for hundreds of years, our accomplishments are nothing short of amazing. What better way to educate and just maybe break a stereotype here or there?

Of course, it takes time to determine who's Jewish and who's not. For the purposes of my collection, "Jewish" means anyone who has at least one Jewish parent and identifies himself as either Jewish or neutral. Converts into the religion count, but converts out of the religion don't. I have to be strict. So Bette Midler, Paul Newman, Joe Lieberman, William Shatner, Jose Bautista, Marilyn Monroe, Yaphet Kotto, Ruth Bader Ginsburg, Goldie Hawn, and Jerry Seinfeld all qualify, but former

Secretary of State Madeleine Albright doesn't since she doesn't consider herself Jewish. After all, I have to have some way to choose who belongs among the Chosen People.

I confirm the Jewishness of everyone in my collection through traditional research and personal contact. A box labeled "Possible Jewish Cards" holds the names of people I suspect might be Jewish. Maybe they have a Jewish-sounding name or I heard a rumor. Sometimes it's pure hunch. As time permits, I write letters and most people reply with signed photos or cards. Even when I'm wrong, most folks are very gracious about my inquiry. Current candidates in the "possible Jewish" category include tough-to-confirm Charlie Chaplin and Telly Savalas.

It's my goal to eventually create a museum—a mini-Smithsonian or as I like to call it, the Smithsteinian—to permanently display this collection of the history of the Jewish people. But in the meantime, I'm always on the lookout for new nominees and acquisitions. If you've got any leads, please let me know.

—*Neil Keller, Maryland*

Photo copyright Bonnie Grube. Used with permission.

The Building Blocks of Life

High-schooler Bonnie Grube was given an assignment to create a piece of art work pertaining to her family and then elaborate about it in an essay. Here she explains how her ancestors not only inspired her work, but also inspire her life.

The reason I chose to put these people in this piece of art is because they are my immediate family who molded and helped create my personality. Each one is an individual who strongly impacted my life and the lives around them.

At the top is a photo of me when I was twelve years old. Below that photo of me are photos of my father and mother. I chose those photos because they depict how I see them in my childhood memories. Below my father and mother are two more pictures of me when I was little. They depict the person-alities of my parents. The photo of me which is below my father's photo shows me smiling, outgoing, and happy, just like my father. The photo of me which is below my mother's photo shows me hiding, but secretly content and happy just like my mother who is more shy than my father.

All the way to the left of the collage is a wedding photo of my grandparents. To the right is a photo of my parents at their wedding. Even though there is a span of about thirty years between the marriages, it shows how we follow in the footsteps of our ancestors. My grandparents got married, my parents got married, and one day I will get married.

In the direct center is another pose of my parents and me, only this time we are all around the same age, reminding me that they were once young like I was. They too played with toys and held the hopes and dreams of all children. As much as sometimes I wish to be different than my parents, this helps me remember that we are all the same.

Right below my parents, as children, in the center, is a photo of my dad when he was about two; further down in the little white dress is my mother also at the age of two. Next to my father as a little boy is my mother's father and on the other side is his future wife, my mother's mother, when she graduated high school. When I graduated high school, I wore a white dress also, just like her.

In the bottom right-hand corner is my mother's father, my mother, and her older sister in the darker dress. My mother's father played a very large role in shaping my mother's person-ality and, in turn, had a big factor in shaping mine through my mother.

In the bottom left-hand corner is a photo of my paternal great-grandparents. My father often mentions them in his childhood memories and, even though I never met them, I feel as if I know them through my father.

At the very bottom slightly to the left of center is a group of family members and in the very center is a little boy who would become  the father of the direct line of ancestors that leads right up to me. His is the oldest ancestor's photo I have and perhaps the influence of his teachings to his children is found somewhere inside of me.

The reason I laid out my collage in the shape of a pyramid is because my ancestors are the building blocks of my life. Each one helped shape and create who I am. They hold me up and I am very proud and thankful for them. Their silhouettes are in the background to show how their shadows and spirits are always with me—maybe through a song of my childhood, or a favorite saying, or maybe even my smile.

—*Bonnie Grube, age 18, New Jersey*

Photo courtesy of the North Carolina Collection, The University of North Carolina at Chapel Hill Libraries. Used with permission.

As American as Siamese Twins

Chang and Eng, joined by a band of cartilage at the base of the breastbone, were born on May 11, 1811 in what was then Siam, now Thailand. Taken by a foreign trader to New York for exhibition and billed as "The Siamese Double Boys," the brothers were permanently associated with their physical condition and country of origin.

Most people's impression and knowledge of the twins begins and ends with P.T. Barnum and his exhibitions, but we descendants of Chang and Eng know them for the men they were—farmers who raised their twenty-one children in Mount Airy, North Carolina—a place so quintessentially American that its other major claim to fame is serving as the model for Mayberry, the hometown of television's Andy Griffith.

As the great-great-granddaughter of Eng, I'd like more people to know the real Chang and Eng. In 1839, disenchanted with touring to make other people wealthy, they took a much needed break. Nearing their thirties, Chang and Eng decided to settle down; they found North Carolina to their liking. They felt it was a place where they could live as normally as possible, where they could just be treated like everyone else. In short order, they adopted the surname of Bunker, applied for American citizenship, and married sisters Adelaide and Sallie Yates.

Chang and Adelaide went on to have ten children, while my great-great-grandparents had eleven. Patriotic Eng named his firstborn son Stephen Decatur after the celebrated naval commander, and both men saw their eldest sons serve in the Civil War for the Confederacy. They donated land and helped build a Baptist church that still stands today. It is there that they were buried when they died in 1874. Theirs, in short, is a story typical of many nineteenth-century American immigrants.

In 1989, 150 years after the twins' arrival in the United States, a Thai television producer contacted one of Chang's great-grandsons and asked about the possibility of assembling Bunker descendants in Surry County, North Carolina, for a documentary that was being filmed. The resulting reunion a year later attracted 175 people. So successful was the event that it quickly became an annual affair and has continued to grow with each passing year.

All of the descendants contribute in their own way. Jessie Bunker Bryant and Milton Haynes were among the original organizers and Jessie recently published an extensive genealogy, *The Connected Bunkers, Descendants of the Siamese Twins Eng and*

1850 Census image of Chang and Eng from Ancestry.com. Used with permission.

Chang Bunker. Betty Bunker Blackmon named the meeting room of her hotel the Bunker Room and decorated it with memorabilia of her famous great-grandfather and his brother. Margaret McNeely recently had one of the twins' specially designed double chairs appraised on the PBS series, *Antiques Roadshow*.

For my own part, I attend the annual Bunker family reunion on the last Saturday in July and urge others to come. This past year, I worked with the Department of Transportation in this area to have the bridge that straddles Stewart's Creek, the body of water that separated their two farms (the twins divided their time between their farms), named in honor of Eng and Chang. The dedication ceremony for the Bunker Bridge was held during this year's reunion.

I encouraged our local visitors center and chamber of commerce to develop an exhibit, and have spoken with numerous reporters, visitors, and book clubs about the lives of the twins. My latest project is to help the producers of *Chang and Eng*, the longest running musical in Singapore's history, to bring the show to the United States after it completes its tour of Thailand, Malaysia, and Hong Kong. While I'm usually wary about books and other works based on my ancestors' lives, I traveled to both Singapore and Bangkok to see the musical and was so impressed that I brought the director, composer, and playwright of the production to this year's reunion in North

Carolina. In terms of interest and fascination, it's hard to improve on the truth, but these men have created a show that does a remarkable job of portraying our rich Bunker history and heritage.

I am very proud to be a descendant of men who were so successful in overcoming adversity. They turned a weakness into a strength and overcame incredible economic, language, and cultural barriers to become successful in their community, businesses, and family lives. They may not have had any choice about being permanently bound to one another, but it is their decidedly American legacy—the lesson that each of us should attempt to make the most of what God gives us—that will keep their more than 1,500 descendants connected forever.

—*Tanya Rees, North Carolina*

The Silent Ones

My CD, *The Silent Ones*, is the fulfillment of my lifelong dream and has taken me on an odyssey of self discovery to Scotland's isle of Lewis, the Eastern Townships of Quebec, and finally, to the main location of the story, Huron Township, Bruce County, Ontario. In music and song, it tells a tale of tragedy and triumph, chronicling the migration of 109 families from the island of Lewis in Scotland's Outer Hebrides to the remote backwoods of nineteenth-century Upper Canada.

Victims of a kind of ethnic cleansing known as the Highland Clearances, the Lewis emigrants were evicted from their *crofts* (small farms) in 1851 by landowner James Matheson. The crofters were then transported overseas, where they settled together in a block of farms in Ontario, maintaining their language and culture well into the twentieth century. The group has become known as the Lewis Settlers.

The Silent Ones is especially close to my heart as I am a direct descendant of these Gaelic pioneers. My CD was recorded at my own multi-tract recording facility, located on a plot of land first settled by my great-grandfather and namesake, Angus Macleod. Composing and recording within the picturesque confines of Huron Township, the exact location of most of the events described in *The Silent Ones*, was a constant source of inspiration for me.

My wife and I can step out of our back door and walk along the little stream where my great-grandparents strolled over a century ago; and close by is the Lewis Cemetery, a site I have often frequented for inspiration.

The first time I visited the Lewis Cemetery, I had a very definite feeling that I had been there before. It was almost like an early childhood memory. I asked my father about it and he assured me that I had never been there. I have since put it down to some kind of genetic recall.

During the recording of *The Silent Ones,* I found myself taking long, early morning walks to that 150-year-old cemetery. Along the way I would pass the location of the settlers' first church, which my great-great-grandfather helped build in 1858. I would also go by the ashen grove where the Lewis folk held open air Gaelic church services upon their arrival in the wilderness.

The impetus to tell the story of the Lewis Settlers struck me while I was standing on a lonely windswept stretch of land at the edge of Europe almost four years ago. I had come to Lewis with my aging father to find the village of our ancestors. The trip was very emotional. My father was eighty-eight years old at the time and not in the best of health. I think he wanted to see where his family came from before he passed on. It was a cold and rainy November morning and I found myself surveying the ocean and a tiny collection of ruins that looked more like randomly placed rock piles than former dwellings. With the village in sight and tears dripping down my cheeks from the emotion of the moment, and from the gale force winds pounding off the Atlantic, the motivation to pursue my lifelong dream came like a thunderclap.

Returning to Canada, I picked up stakes and moved to Huron Township. I vowed to tell the story of my family and their forced exile from the ancestral homeland—a story that can be echoed by hundreds of thousands of Canadians of Highland and Island descent. I knew that in order to tell the story, I had to return to the place where images for *The Silent Ones* were first stirred within me some forty years earlier.

My CD is unique in its use of narration and spoken word. The spoken word acts as a thread woven throughout the fabric of the piece, connecting the songs and instrumental music together. Mostly in Gaelic, these sections add a mystical atmosphere. The sixty-four-minute CD was recorded between February 1998 and July 2000 and meticulously combines state-of-the-art keyboard and computer technology with traditional instruments, such as a Highland bagpipe, fiddle, whistle, mandolin, and hammer dulcimer. Vocals are shared by two young female vocalists from Kincardine, Ontario (both of whom are of Highland descent), and myself.

I remember taking a break from recording one evening, stepping outside to catch a breath of night air. I had left the tape machine running and one of the Gaelic portions was drifting out of the studio window, the ancient words of the text bouncing off the trees and floating across the fields down to the tiny stream at the back of our property. In a moment of enlightenment, I realized that these old words, now foreign to the area's residents, had not been spoken here since my great-grandparents' time. As the words echoed carelessly around my great-grandfather's former homestead, I could feel his spirit in the rustling of the trees and the gentle motion of the summer breeze.

I was born into a long line of traditional singers and storytellers. My early memories of my grandfather are of a kindly old gentleman singing in a strange, awkward tongue. At the time, I thought that he was making up his own special language. I was in my teens before my father explained to me that my grandfather was really singing in Gaelic. As a child, I spent my summers in Huron Township where my great-aunts told me stories of a not so distant past—stories about pioneer life in the backwoods of Canada and tales of a far away island off the coast of Scotland. Those early years made a lasting impression on me and have been a constant influence on my life. *The Silent Ones* is the result of my lifelong dream: to tell the story of Huron Township's Lewis Settlers the best way I know, through music.

—*Angus Macleod, Canada, as told to Joan Griffis*

The Battle to Preserve War Letters

I had no particular interest in history or letters until a fire swept through my family's home in Washington, D.C., just before Christmas of 1989. Thankfully, no one was hurt (even Claude, our cat, bounded out safely), but all our possessions were destroyed. As I walked cautiously through the burnt-out shell of our house several days later, it occurred to me that all my letters were gone. The clothes, the furniture, the books, just about everything else could be replaced, but not the letters.

The lost letters were certainly not worthy of the National Archives, they were mostly just correspondences with old girl-friends and high school buddies traveling abroad. But I did have a series of riveting letters by a friend who was in Beijing during the Tiannamen Square massacre in June 1989. It was crushing to realize that his letters, along with the seemingly trivial ones, were now gone.

The fire, which in retrospect was something of a godsend, inspired in me a lifelong passion for letters. And ultimately it triggered the creation of the Legacy Project, a national nonprofit organization I founded in 1998 that encourages Americans to seek out and preserve their family correspondence.

Our focus on war began after I spoke with a handful of veterans who said that they had thrown away their old letters. They were very modest about their service and felt no one would be interested in what they had written. Even more tragically, I discovered that over a thousand veterans are dying every day, and their loved ones were often discarding their letters as well. This was stunning to me. The few war letters I had seen were more emotionally intense and dramatic than anything I had ever read. Composed under life and death circumstances, every letter took on new meaning. Soldiers never knew if that letter would be their last, which often inspired in them greater clarity and poetry of expression. "You don't mince words in a foxhole," one veteran explained to me.

On a whim, I contacted "Dear Abby" and asked her to write a column urging her readers to save their war letters and, if they thought they had something historically significant, to send a photocopy to the Legacy Project. "Dear Abby" agreed, and the column appeared on November 11, 1998—Veterans Day.

Three days later, a clerk at the post office called. "Is this Andrew Carroll?" he asked testily. I said that it was. "You need

187

to come down here now and get your mail." I assured the clerk that I would hop on my bike and be there in minutes. "Bring a car," he said, and hung up. He wasn't kidding.

Bins and bins of letters were pouring in. I immediately tore into the envelopes and began reading. Here were eyewitness accounts of Gettysburg and D-Day, Shiloh and Pearl Harbor, the Tet Offensive, Desert Storm, St. Mihiel, and even e-mails from Bosnia. Every war in our nation's history was represented.

I was only three years old when U.S. troops pulled out of Vietnam in 1973, and no one in my immediate family has ever served in the armed forces. Nothing I had ever seen, or read, or been told about war prepared me for what I received. I had braced myself for graphic descriptions of bloodshed and stories of brutality and suffering, and I suspected there would be intimate letters to wives and girlfriends written by forlorn soldiers who, in so many cases, later died in battle. What caught me off guard were the personal messages enclosed with every war letter:

"Dear Sir, Please accept these letters that my brother had written to my mother. My brother is missing (not a POW). He was never right after he returned home and one day he was just gone. I hope to make his life worth something. I miss him very much."

"I am a widow eighty-five years old and my husband and only son have passed. My husband served in Patton's Third Army. There is no one I can give my husband's letters to so you may have them. Please remember him."

Please remember him. Time and time again, the writers pleaded with me to please remember.

Featuring two hundred of the more than 50,000 letters the Legacy Project has received to date, *War Letters: Extraordinary Correspondence from American Wars*, was born. Because we had promised that the Legacy Project would not profit from the letters sent, all of my earnings from the book are being donated to veterans groups.

We continue to solicit more letters and will eventually create a Web-based archive and distribute some of the original letters to appropriate museums and collections. Our true mission, though, is to prevent the disposal of this great, unknown literature of the American people. Please remember and acknowledge the veterans in your family or local community by protecting their letters or donating them to a reputable museum, archive, library, or historical society so that future generations will have access to and can learn from these irreplaceable documents. Together, we can keep these letters—which are truly the pages of our national autobiography—from disappearing forever.

—*Andrew Carroll, Washington, DC*

To learn more about the Legacy Project, visit www.warletters.com.

Collecting Answers

When Albert Einstein was awarded the Nobel Prize in 1921, it was for "important work carried out in 1905." There was no mention of relativity, because of the swirling controversy surrounding his work. Even respected scientists stood opposed to his theory and thought Einstein was wrong.

Today, there are educated Americans who stand opposed to collecting enslavement period materials. These hypersensitive, squeamish people believe Sam Pittman is wrong. They do not understand how important it is to establish the context in which Africans were kidnapped and sold in the Americas. They do not understand the importance of collecting evidence that marks how slaves endured and persevered to enrich and shape our national character and culture.

I never deliberately formulated a plan to collect enslavement period materials as a tribute, but upon reflection, I can trace the origins of my collection to my desire to understand
- the roots of slavery in general,
- the Trans-Atlantic slave trade in particular, and
- the reasons it took 300 years and a civil war to rid America of slavery.

It was this quest that led me to my first Black memorabilia auction. My wife, who tolerated my persistent, almost obnoxious questioning, heard about an auction in New Jersey and thought it would be a good idea for me to go. The first item presented was a "jolly nigger bank," which sold for $300. I decided that was outrageous and waited for the next item, which turned out to be a grotesque image of an African American woman called "Diana." Selling for more than $400, Diana became the first item in my collection. I walked away that day with a receipt of $5,000. That was my baptism to collecting.

After that first experience, my wife said she would never take me out of New York again, but each summer, I would travel all over the South and seek out flea markets and auctions. I knew the answers I was looking for couldn't be found in libraries.

Now, decades later, my collection includes all kinds of shackles and slave collars dating back as far as the 1730s, more than 40,000 books about or by African Americans, stamps and covers, cereal boxes with African Americans, entertainment dolls, hundreds of copies of *The Liberator*, every issue of Frederick Douglass's *Paper*, and even a tusk carving with the history of the trans-Atlantic slave trade on it, one of only three known in the world. I also collect coins and currency with Africans on them and am writing a book called *You're on the Money* about African Americans whose images or signatures are found on American currency.

As to my questions, my collection has helped me find answers:

The origins of slavery come from the ancient philosophy of "to the victor go the spoils." Thousands of years ago, when warriors captured a village, they would kill their captives. But about 3,000 years ago, someone got the bright idea that they should be a little more liberal and give the vanquished the choice of public execution or a life of labor without pay. Thus, the origin of slavery.

Ironically, the trans-Atlantic slave trade is rooted in compassion. A Catholic priest named Bartholomew de la Casa realized that the Spaniards who had come to the New World in search of gold were about to make the indigenous people extinct if they didn't stop working them to death in the gold mines. Out of mercy for the Indians, he suggested the substitution of African labor for Indian labor. Shortly thereafter, the first load of Africans was taken to the New World. This was the trigger for the barbaric trans-Atlantic slave trade that ensued.

As to my last question, our founding fathers never wanted slavery in the United States, even though many of them were slave owners themselves. The need to compromise with politicians from the Southern states resulted in the inclusion of several pro-slavery clauses in the United States Constitution. These proved to be a cancer surgically implanted in our infant nation. Although this very sick infant did not die, she hemorrhaged for seventy-five years until Major Anderson hauled down our flag at Fort Sumter.

The cure to slavery was costly. It took a civil war and a million deaths. Armed with this knowledge, I am a living tribute to our ancestors, like those who died at Fort Pillow in the Civil War or those who marched even earlier with Dunmore's Royal Ethiopian Regiment in the American Revolution. It is an awareness of these and countless other deeds with which I so closely identify. Sometimes I believe that my ancestors and I are one and the same. Our ancestors are my spiritual self.

I occasionally get negative reactions to my slavery collection, only because people don't know the history themselves. Even historians have not lived up to their code of objectivity; their writings have been mainly distorted. Therefore, African Americans had no way of understanding their history or their contribution to history to answer the question, "Who am I?" Fortunately, that's been changing in our society since the 1960s and now young people are more knowledgeable. American history is being rewritten to show that it really is African American history; you can't separate them.

After years of searching and collecting, I am satisfied with the answers I've found and can now close my eyes and join my ancestors in their "dirt nap" anytime. I pay tribute to them through my collection, but in a larger sense, I pay tribute and honor by simply having the knowledge of who I am and who they were.

—*Sample Pittman, Ph.D, New York*

The Wind
at My Back

Although I consider myself a spiritual person, I haven't been overly involved in organized religion as an adult. My skepticism in the existence of a "hereafter" was turned upside-down, however, one hot September day, alone in a small North Carolina cemetery. At least I thought I had been alone.

Following a work-related trip to Virginia, I headed south on a Sunday morning to visit the region my Bain ancestors had helped settle when they emigrated from Scotland. Long before dawn I set out for Wade, North Carolina. An aunt of mine had discovered a Bain family history in the North Carolina State Archives several years before. John Corinth Bain (1862–1930) had written and published the little booklet in 1928, and it detailed the family relations back to our arrival in the Wade area in 1740.

Because of my hobby of flying stunt kites, I made note of the wind levels that morning. As in the previous week in Virginia, there was none, not even the four or five mile per hour puffs required for my lightweight stunt kite. No matter. I was on a mission to the town of Wade, in Cumberland County, and the Old Bluff Presbyterian Church awaited me.

A small dirt road wound through the cemetery, past the old, white clapboard church, and back to the entrance. I was not alone; many other people were paying their respects to their own loved ones that Sunday. I spent the better part of the afternoon in the cemetery, busily photographing dozens of Bain headstones, jotting down information that might not be legible in photographs, and noting family groupings. Among the ancestors, I found John C. Bain buried there, several dozen yards from the church on the bluff over the Cape Fear River.

Late into the evening in my hotel room, I transcribed my scribbled notes, examined my charts, and made connections between individuals and families that hadn't been so apparent in the cemetery. There were one or two individuals I was surprised not to find at Old Bluff and I assumed that they were probably buried in small family plots nearby.

The next morning turned out to be as hot and windless as the week before. I jumped in the car, heading down a country road toward I-95. For some reason, I couldn't quite get myself to turn onto the highway, although I tried several times; I wasn't comfortable with the thought of leaving Wade. After a while, I found myself back at the end of the dirt road that led to the Old Bluff Presbyterian Church and cemetery. I reasoned that I might as

195

John C. Bain, author of the family record that ultimately brought the author to the cemetery

well stop by for a quick farewell to my ancestors, not knowing when I might be back in this part of the country.

As I drove into the cemetery grounds, I noticed there was no one else there (of course not, I thought, it's Monday morning). I parked as close to John C. Bain's plot as possible, leaving my camera gear and notes in the car. This was to be a quick walk through the cemetery, as I had completed my research the day before.

I'm not sure why, but I often speak out loud in cemeteries, greeting those deceased family members I'm visiting, and asking the pardon of the individuals whose plots I may be inadvertently crossing. I have always done so, partially out of respect for the graves and hallowed ground I am visiting, partly out of a feeling that in some way, my words might be heard. Alone now, I spoke to several of the family groupings, introducing myself and wishing them a peaceful rest.

Standing in front of one family cluster of headstones, I noticed a smaller stone on the edge of the property, almost in the woods. Not remembering it from the day before, I walked over to see who might be buried in such an out-of-the-way place. I found the grave of Catherine Graham Bain, the mother who was conspicuously missing from the nearby family grouping.

"Catherine! What are you doing over here?" I blurted out. "Your whole family is over there! Did something happen?"

I'm not sure why I asked that last question, but I immediately heard a low rumbling, almost what I imagine a low-level earthquake would sound like. I looked in vain to the sky for distant jets or for wind that might have made this sound. The hair on the back of my neck stood up and I backed away, muttering, "Okay, that's fine, I was just curious, and I hope that whatever the reason, you're resting in peace." I tried to convince myself that there must be a logical explanation for the rumbling sound.

Back near John C. Bain's gravestone, I stood ready to depart. He had been a rural mail carrier, and it was easy to picture him making his daily rounds. I thanked him (aloud, of course) for all of his years of research and for taking the time and trouble to publish his booklet some sixty years earlier, the work that eventually compelled me to visit the Old Bluff cemetery. I said goodbye, and stretching out my arms, I looked around and bid farewell to all the ancestors with whom I had visited during these two days.

And then the wind came.

Out of nowhere, a very strong wind whipped up behind me. My eyes widened and looking up, I saw the tops of the seventy-five-foot tall pine trees pitching to and fro. The wind was coming from straight behind me, pushing my hair forward into my face. More than just a feeling, I knew that this was some type of message from my collective ancestors, scores of whom were buried there. I felt no fear whatsoever, just the most heartfelt connection, as if these distant relatives were thanking me for acknowledging them, thanking me for remembering them, thanking me for continuing the family record. They were sending me on my way, with the wind at my back.

After fifteen to twenty seconds, the wind calmed down substantially, yet my wonder at the events remained high; I was almost giddy. I earnestly thanked them all, especially John, for that wonderful gift. I kept chuckling and looking

Photos by Christopher C. Bain. Used with permission.

back, almost in disbelief, as I reluctantly walked over to the car and slowly drove out of the cemetery. Just outside of the front gates I stopped the car and got out for one last look over the cemetery as I had first seen it when I had driven in the day before. The entire scene was utterly windless, as still and peaceful as a photograph. Yet the difference I felt was profound.

I had no trouble driving onto the highway then; my business in Wade was now complete. I traveled to Whiteville that day, in search of my grandfather and great-grandfather's resting place, and didn't experience a puff of wind until I approached the Wilmington airport the next evening, as I was departing North Carolina.

Before this experience, I hadn't believed in anything I couldn't see or touch. Talk of the hereafter and stories of "other world" experiences often brought a smirk to my face. But the ancestral connection I had that day at the Old Bluff cemetery forced me to reconsider and open my mind to that which I can't necessarily explain. Other hard-to-explain events that have subsequently occurred during trips to family cemeteries have reinforced my new beliefs. As long as they encourage me with wayward winds and other unspoken messages, I'll continue seeking out and talking to my ancestors.

—*Christopher C. Bain, New York*

Logo courtesy of Mari Modlin. Used with permission.

Accepting Black Sheep into the Fold

Iam Flockmaster to a very select group of people, and while more than five thousand Society memberships have now been granted, only those with the right credentials need bother to apply. We only accept those who can prove direct descent from at least one notorious ancestor. More specifically, applicants must substantiate that they have ancestors who were involved in at least one of the following:

• Murder
• Kidnapping
• Armed robbery
• Treason
• Theft of any item of fame
• Membership in a famous gang

- Political assassin
- Inclusion on the FBI's most wanted list
- Political expatriation
- Extreme public embarrassment
- Involvement in witchcraft trials
- Bigamy
- Expulsion from normal society (expelled, excommunicated, deported, and "warned out")
- Felony conviction
- Transportation to a convict colony

Other situations may qualify for membership in the International Black Sheep Society of Genealogists on a case-by-case basis, and recent or close family involvement can qualify privately through our Tender Lambs Program. But our strict rules do not allow an applicant to qualify under his own activities.

Yes, I realize this may sound a bit elitist or exclusionary at first, but if you think about it, there's a proverbial black sheep in every family. And families tend to deal with them in one of two ways. Either they embrace them for the color and character they add to the family tree or they hide them in shame.

In the latter case, having a black sheep in the family leads to a wall of silence making genealogical research very difficult. I learned this first-hand when I decided to try to locate my father's missing family. Dad had no contact with his family since 1945, the year his father passed away. It took me until 1998 to trace my father's lost family, including seven siblings he had never met.

It was this experience that led me several years ago to join an online discussion about the ancestral blockages created by silent relatives. Before long, a large group of us were exchanging stories of black sheep ancestors and relatives who left out whole branches of the family tree or even changed names to avoid being associated with the infamous individual.

By early 1998, there were so many of us that I started a mailing list, officially launched the International Black Sheep Society of Genealogists, and assumed the position of Flockmaster.

The purpose of our Society is to help find alternate routes to information sources when those walls of silence spring up, and to promote the view of the black sheep as a person who has a place in the factual history of the family, without regard to behavior.

Why bring the family's dirty laundry out to wash? Simply put, the laundry needs to be aired, and once it is, there is no "stain" of shame remaining. The family can rid themselves of self-imposed stress over what someone has done and return to normalcy.

The Society feels it's all just history. Whatever may have occurred, it is but one facet of a person's life, and although that one factor may have changed the black sheep's life path, it is just a fact that should be reported as such. Only then can progress be made in researching the family prior to this obstacle.

So if your Pilgrim forebear was sentenced to be whipped at the public post for "uncleanliness with his wife before marriage," or your ancestor killed a local policeman in a battle over moonshine, or your great-grandmother was a high society con woman, you're not alone. Within the Society we can all relate, so there's absolutely nothing to feel sheepish about.

—*Jeffery Scism, California*

To learn more about the International Black Sheep Society of Genealogists, visit www.blacksheep.rootsweb.com.

The Legacy

While sitting on my bed, surrounded by old photo albums, scrapbooks, newspapers, and remembrances of a time long ago, I thought back to the day my dad asked me to take on the task of researching our family history. I recalled my thrill when he arrived carrying boxes filled to the brim with photos I'd never before seen. Within these photos and mementos was a documented history of my ancestors—people I'd never known, but who, within me and my DNA makeup, continued on. My search to know them brought me to where I now sat, several years later, on my bed amidst a sea of clues without answers.

With a feeling of perseverance, I went back to the beginning, looking at things I'd seen time and time again. Picking up a photo of Mary Stever, my great grandmother, I smiled at the expression on her face and truly studied her image, noting details I'd overlooked before. I saw details like the wisps of hair escaping from the constrained bun she tried to subdue them within, and the hint of a dimple in her chin—a sign of stubbornness, perhaps? I noted that her stiff upright posture was belied by the twinkle in her eyes, and the suppressed laughter that threatened to spill from behind her gently smiling lips. The dress she wore was neatly tailored and pressed, its only adornment was the long watch chain that crossed her chest and ended neatly tucked at her waist. Looking at Mary, I felt as if I were truly seeing her for the first time. And then there was her scrapbook of poems with its images of children, flowers, and animals. All of these combined to make me feel as if I truly knew her. No longer was she just a name on my family tree. She was Mary. My Mary.

At one point in time, my dad told me about his grandparents, Mary Stever and William Henry Watson. "Theirs was the love of a lifetime," he had said. He knew because after the deaths of his grandparents, he and Mom moved into the Watson family home. And it was there, tucked back into a cupboard's recess, that he and Mom discovered many old love letters that had been exchanged between Mary and Henry. As Dad and Mom began reading the letters, they each had a feeling of trespassing—their eyes were reading words that had been meant only for Mary or Henry. So without further ado, Dad and Mom destroyed the letters.

Although that act is something my now eighty-two-year-old father regrets, we both realize it was an act done out of love and respect—for his grandparents and even for the love he and my mother shared between themselves. Thinking of that love, and how it carried Mary across the country from her home in Illinois to a new life in Oregon, I was suddenly filled with an outpouring of words.

I admit there have been many times when I've expressed myself by writing poems, putting to paper my emotions and thoughts, but this experience was like no other. I can honestly say I had chills and felt the hair stand up on the back of my neck. All I knew was that I had to find paper and pencil to write down what was pouring into my thoughts. I began to write, scribbling as fast as I could, trying to keep up with the gushing flow of rhyming words.

It was only when that constant flow of words stopped that I picked up the paper with a shaking hand and, for the first time, read and realized the actual message in those words. Eventually, the poem found its way to the Internet, where it was and remains posted to a popular website. Since then, I've received several hundred e-mails from people who read the poem and somehow connected to it. Some people said they'd been frustrated in their genealogical search, ready to quit, but then felt inspired to continue their search for their heritage after having read the poem. Others said it was just as their grandparents had described it—their emotions and reasons for seeking passage to America. Still others simply wrote and said "beautiful" or "thank you."

As strange as it might sound, I don't for a moment believe the words of this poem were of my making. I gave the poem a title, no more. Instead, I feel that I was simply the messenger and the poem was a gift to be shared—from those whose voices will not be silenced by time.

—Rebecca Watson Walker, Oregon

The Legacy

Voices of a distant time
Speak softly through the years
Carried on winds of ages past
Whispering gently in our ears.

Seeking to be remembered
Rather than forgotten as though never here,
Reaching out to their children's children...
"Do they listen? Will they hear?"

From far off lands and distant seas
With courage and fear interlaced,
They sought a new future for their children,
But unsure of the future they faced.

They arrived at port as families,
As well as lone woman or man.
Even a child or infant would travel
To the promise of that other land.

Hazards of travel, whether land or sea
Would claim both young and old.
This new land would hold a price for some,
But undaunted, forward they'd go.

Far from what they once called home
They embraced this new found land.
Though their hearts recalled it, they'd still proudly
Proclaim it: "I'm an American."

Though many to America were penniless
With nought but their Bible to hold,
They knew therein lie a treasure:
Joys and sorrows, recorded and told.

Each name seems to say: "Don't forget me;
please remember those things we endured.
We risked it all; life, home, love and family,
so your future would be secured."

Epilogue

Show me the manner in which a nation cares for its dead, and I will measure with mathematical exactness the tender mercies of its people, their respect for the laws of the land and their loyalty to high ideals.

—William Gladstone (1809–98)

These words were spoken long ago, but they still ring true today. And if the preceding stories are any indication, it seems there's hope for us yet! Those ancestors who voice their fears of being forgotten in *The Legacy*—"Do they listen? Will they hear?"—can rest in the assurance that they are indeed being remembered and celebrated. More and more of us are reaching for our roots and tuning into our ancestral inheritance. And once we find it, we use it as a source of inspiration and direction, as a means to connect, and as a path to self-discovery.

We show our gratitude for these gifts by creatively honoring our ancestors in a thousand different ways, but in case you're still not quite convinced of this quiet phenomenon—or just haven't found the approach that's right for you—I leave you with this remarkably diverse menu of actual ancestral tributes:

- Mayflower descendant Richard Pickering delivers lectures in the colonial-era English used by the pilgrims, while amazing his audiences by changing from modern clothing to pilgrim-wear before their eyes.

- Stephen Lignowski cross-stitched a portrait of his great-grandmother, Henrietta Branch Oliver, to present to his grandmother as a gift. The portrait, which measures eleven by eighteen inches and has a stitch density of 484 stitches per square inch, took him five years to complete.

- The Poorhouse Story (www.poorhousestory.com) is a website started by Linda Crannell after she began researching her great-great-grandmother who had lived in a poorhouse. Her intent is to make records of nineteenth-century American poorhouses accessible for research, to remove the secrecy that shrouds the poorhouse, and to dispel the negative image attached to poorhouse residence.

- Ron Howard directed *Far and Away* at least partly as a tribute to his own immigrant roots and the three of his great-grandparents who participated in the 1893 Oklahoma Land Race.

- Eve Richardson participated in an archaeological dig at a church cemetery in England and was given the honor of naming one of the skeletons unearthed after one of her ancestors.

- Scott Stanton scours the world finding the burial sites of musicians of all stripes. His book *The Tombstone Tourist* records the locations, notes the inscriptions, and provides additional data.

- More than 1,200 descendants of the thirty-six Cape Hatteras Lighthouse keepers, who protected North Carolina's Outer Banks shores from 1803 to 1939, recently gathered for a reunion and unveiling of a memorial to their ancestors.

- Life coach Anna Grace Harding conducts a workshop called "All My Grandmothers" to help women explore and celebrate their deep connections to their grandmothers.

- Kristi Murdock of Iowa gathered a collection of letters her grandparents had exchanged during World War I and self-published them. To ensure their preservation, she is donating the book to several appropriate historical societies.

- The eleventh Earl of Sandwich recently helped his son launch a gourmet sandwich delivery service in London named—you guessed it—Earl of Sandwich. It was his ancestor, the fourth Earl of Sandwich, who is said to have introduced the world to the then new-fangled food some 240 years ago.

- Irene Jeppsen makes coloring books of her forebears to help younger family members get to know their predecessors.

- Harriett Robards-Lott grew up in Mexico where many villages hold a Day of the Dead festival each November to celebrate the memory of the deceased and pray for their souls. Parades lead to and from cemeteries, which are cleaned and adorned with flowers and candles for the occasion, and picnics and specially prepared candies are enjoyed by all.

- Irish-American Mayor Martin O'Malley of Baltimore, Maryland, leaves political pressures behind when performing with his Celtic rock band "O'Malley's March."

- Parents of children adopted from China and Vietnam are forming groups that meet periodically for festivals and other events designed to help their children learn about and celebrate their heritage.

- When she married in 2000, Elizabeth Kennedy's reception incorporated a "Table of Ancestors" featuring several generations of family wedding photos and announcements.

- Karen Sutton and Kathy Thompson launched an oral history project to identify and interview descendants of slaves held by Nathaniel Burwell II at Carter's Grove Plantation near colonial Williamsburg in Virginia.

- Questioned as to why he made the film *Dudley Do-Right*, actor Brendan Fraser replied, "My great-grandfather was a Canadian Mounted Policemen. I would have regretted not making a Mountie movie if I had the chance."

- Frustrated with the deplorable condition of the Delaware Public Archives, Jacqueline Skinner organized a petition drive to collect more than five thousand signatures to convince the state to rectify the situation. The result? A new $18 million, 80,000 square-foot facility.

- Gail Lumet Buckley, daughter of Lena Horne, researched and wrote *The Hornes* about her own family. Later, after coming across her grandfather's trunk of family treasures and learning about a great-uncle Errol who had served in a "buffalo soldier" cavalry regiment, she was inspired to devote fourteen years digging into other families' trunks to write *American Patriots: The Story of Blacks in the Military from the Revolution to Desert Storm*, a book that tells the largely ignored story of black soldiers.

- Nancy Lublin established Dress for Success with a $5,000 inheritance from her altruistic, immigrant great-grandfather. The charity, created in his honor, provides professional clothing for women who might not otherwise be able to obtain it.

- Drew Barrymore draws inspiration from the numerous photos of her famous Barrymore kin adorning the walls in her offices at Flower Films.

- Finally given a chance in 2000 to reclaim their surnames (banished seventy-five years earlier by the Soviets as part of the effort to squash the local culture), Mongolians demonstrated extreme pride in their national identity when more than sixty percent, believing themselves to be of the same lineage as Genghis Khan, considered adopting

211

his surname of Borjigon. A special study was undertaken to unearth more than 1,300 forgotten Mongolian surnames in an attempt to persuade people to select other surnames.

- John and Helen Cartales of Washington commissioned a mural of John's immigrant father's village in Greece over the winding staircase in their home. Villagers in the scene have the faces of John's relatives which the artist was able to reproduce from old family photos.

- Ann Mix founded the American World War II Orphans Network (www.awon.org) to help those orphaned by the war learn about the fathers most of them never knew.

- William Crockett, great-great-great-great-grandnephew of Davy Crockett, adds to his stash of lunch boxes, cookie jars, and other collectibles commemorating his famous ancestor by participating in online auctions.

- Irving Chais keeps his family tradition alive by being the third generation to run the New York Doll Hospital that administers treatment to dolls with ailments of all kinds.

- Paul McCartney and his companion Heather Mills recently bought a graveyard in Croatia as part of the United Nations' Adopt-a-Minefield campaign. Once the graveyard has been cleared of landmines, McCartney explains that the people who live in that village will be able to "walk in that field and tend their ancestors' graves."

- Storyteller and Appalachian folkways preserver Kathy Coleman blends tales, tunes, quilts, and mountain folk toys into programs such as Appalachian Tales and Tunes, Patchwork Tales, and Voices of Virginia. Thousands of listeners in hundreds of venues have enjoyed her spirited cultural reminders.

- Mary Ann Allen's searchable website, Photographs from the Past (www.photographsfromthepast.com/index.html), is dedicated to reuniting mystery photos she and others have found in antiques stores and flea markets with their families of origin.

- "I've always been fascinated by the concept of being a reflection of our ancestors and reflecting who was there before us," said rapper Talib Kweli, discussing the inspiration behind his and DJ Hi Tek's release *Train of Thought*. Lyrics from the song "Africa Dream" underscore this theme: "Yo, we the reflection of our ancestors. We'd like to thank you for the building blocks you left us. Cause your spirit possessed us. Yo, you blessed us. Thank you very much..."

- In 2000, Paul Michael drove a horse and buggy the 130 miles from Lyons, Kansas, to Deer Creek, Oklahoma, retracing his grandfather's ride in the Cherokee Strip in 1893.

- The unveiling of The Tower of Freedom, a monument honoring Caroline Quarrelles and other slaves who escaped to freedom in Canada, was attended by descendants of

Quarrelles. She was only sixteen in 1842 when she ran away from Missouri and made her way via the Underground Railroad to Milwaukee and finally to Canada.

- Ukrainian immigrant Maria Wowk spent over a year decorating two thousand real eggs in the traditional pysanky style in honor of the new millennium and her heritage.

- In a program she calls "Finding and Honoring Our Spanish-Mexican Grandmothers," Gloria Cordova uses her own family history and doctoral dissertation research as a means of discovering and giving visibility to Spanish-mestiza ancestral women, particularly those early Hispano settlers of what is now New Mexico.

- Among other tributes to his heritage and history, Steven Spielberg created the masterful *Schindler's List* and spearheaded the Shoah Foundation efforts to collect more than fifty thousand oral histories of Holocaust survivors. Less well known is the fact that Feivel, the immigrant mouse featured in the animated *American Tail* movies, was named after his grandfather.

Here's wishing you the best in your quest, however you choose to honor your ancestors!

I, _____, have decided to

_____ to pay tribute to

_____.

Permissions

"The Tower of Life" by Yaffa Eliach is reprinted with permission from *Sh'ma: A Journal of Jewish Responsibility*, June 2001, 31:583, pages 11–12. For more information about Sh'ma visit www.shma.com.

"Blending Research and Photographs to Paint a Portrait of an Ancestral Home," written by Pamelia Schwannecke Olson, appeared in the September/October 1991 issue of *Heritage Quest*, issue #36, pages 50–51. Reprinted by permission.

"Unknown Soldiers Identified by DNA from Their Female Lines," written by Megan Smolenyak, appeared in the May/June 2001 issue of *Heritage Quest*, Volume 17, Number 3, pages 34–38. Reprinted by permission.

"Appointment in Ghana," written by Reneé Kemp, appeared in the July-August 2000 issue of *Modern Maturity*, Volume 43W, Number 4, pages 17–29. Reprinted by permission.

Excerpt from *So Mourns the Dove*, edited by Alto Loftin Jackson, Exposition Press: New York, 1965, used in "Beholden" with permission.

"Coincidence: Serendipitous Events at the Cemetery," written by Christopher C. Bain, appeared in the September/October 2001 issue of *Ancestry*, Volume 19, Number 5, pages 34-38. Reprinted by permission.

The cover of DEAR AMERICA: A COAL MINER'S DIARY by Susan Campbell Bartoletti, Copyright © 2001 by Susan Campbell Bartoletti, is used by permission of Scholastic Inc. DEAR AMERICA is a registered trademark of Scholastic Inc. Cover portrait: Sergei Mikhailovich Prokudin-Gorskii, Library of Congress. Cover background: Paul Thomas Studio, Shamokin, Pennsylvania.

Photo by Cole Goodwin

About the Author

Megan Smolenyak Smolenyak (yes, that's her real name) has been an avid genealogist for more than thirty years and is skilled in many aspects of family history. As lead researcher for the 2000 PBS Ancestors series, she delved into over five thousand genealogical stories and wrote the companion book, *In Search of Our Ancestors: 101 Inspiring Stories of Serendipity and Connection in Rediscovering Our Family History*.

Since 2000, Megan has been a consultant with the U.S. Army's Repatriation project to trace families of servicemen killed or Missing In Action in Korea, World War II, and Vietnam. She has supported this and many other genealogical initiatives through her Honoring Our Ancestors grants program.

A contributing editor for *Heritage Quest*, Megan has appeared on the *Today Show, Fox & Friends, Ancestors,* and *NPR* among others, and has spoken at numerous conferences. Formerly an international marketing consultant, she has traveled to all the continents and has degrees in Foreign Service, International Business, and Information Technology.

Megan lives in Virginia with her husband, Brian, whom she met through her genealogical research! To contact her, apply for an Honoring Our Ancestors grant, or share your experiences, visit www.honoringourancestors.com.